ONE LIFE TO LOVE

Vinaya Patil, an ex-IT employee, is an electronics engineer by qualification. She is now a full-time writer. She is also a theatre enthusiast and has acted in several plays.

ONE LIFE TO LOVE

Vinaya Patil

RUPA

Published by
Rupa Publications India Pvt. Ltd 2014
7/16, Ansari Road, Daryaganj
New Delhi 110002

Sales centres:
Allahabad Bengaluru Chennai
Hyderabad Jaipur Kathmandu
Kolkata Mumbai

ISBN: 978-81-291-3109-6

First impression 2014

10 9 8 7 6 5 4 3 2 1

The moral right of the author has been asserted.

Typeset by Saanavi Graphics, Noida

Printed at Gopsons Papers Ltd., Noida

I dedicate this book to my late Mother-in-law, Ashwini Patil, who read the first draft and had only nice things to say about it. Mom, it is because of your blessings that the book is in print.

Contents

A Lot can Happen Over Dosa

'Stop! Stop! Saachi! Stop!'

I brought the Scooty to a screeching halt, turning in panic, 'What...!'

Riya clambered off the pillion and pointed to a canary yellow bike parked in front of the cafeteria.

'What...?' I asked bewildered. Riya, meanwhile, was scrabbling about in her handbag and triumphantly pulled out a comb. 'He's in there,' she said, running the comb through her hair. 'Who?' I asked, exasperated. 'Him,' she replied simply. I had no idea who 'Him' was, and I am her best friend. But the way she said it...

Before I could get any more out of her, Riya had rushed towards the cafeteria. I trudged after her. Her attendance was choppy and Prof. Sharada wouldn't take too kindly to her bunking class. Our exams were round the corner—not that it mattered to Riya—but it did to me.

As I parked the Scooty before heading to the cafeteria after Riya, I sighed. It had been such a nice tranquil morning. The flowers were riotously in bloom all over campus, in fact all across Bengaluru. I had been soaking it all in, driving us to college. And now this! Riya rushing into the cafeteria after someone who rode a flashy yellow bike.

I made another attempt to stop her. 'Riya, wait! I don't think we should bunk.'

'Saachi, babe, please understand. It is "Hunk" over "Hertz", "Love" over "Lectures" on boring subjects which have never made sense, "Cute guy" over "Circuits" which can jam your brain or short circuit it, which can be even worse.' She spoke with conviction expressing her fake interest in electronics engineering the subject she had chosen. She had made up her mind.

By now she was probably dreaming about having children and grandchildren with him. I wanted to shake her, tell her to grow up, but I could never bring myself to hurt Riya.

I had my reasons. Riya is the only and somewhat lonely daughter of one of Bengaluru's richest men. Her parents separated when she was quite young, and her mother moved to London. Riya lived with her father in the very upmarket locale of Sadashivnagar, while I lived with my folks in Malleshwaram, one of Bengaluru's oldest and staunchly middle-class localities.

The sanctity of our four-year-long friendship was maintained by the fact that when we were together, money, status and other assorted rubbish went out of the window. Our bond transcended the golden cage she lived in. Riya, to me, was my best friend. I knew her shortcomings as well as her innumerable good qualities. And so, I loyally trudged to the cafeteria in search of Riya. She stood waiting for me by the far wall, her eyes shining with a thousand dreams.

The canteen was not bathed in any such roseate glow. It looked decrepit, just as it had for the last three years. The washed-out colour of its walls made a sorry background for posters of F1 cars. Plastic chairs were strewn around tables. The tabletops had names lovingly scratched into them by besotted boys, listing a 'who's who' of the most beautiful girls in the city. Wannabe artists had established their credentials by carving tiny nude women on the plastic tabletops. And there were people like Riya who existed unperturbed in this whacko world. Money probably made for very comfortable blinders.

My thoughts were interrupted by the sharp nudge of an elbow. 'Check out the table at 3:15,' hissed Riya. I turned my eyes discreetly to the right. Her hero was dazzling alright. His hair shone and glistened, slicked back with a tubeful of gel, and Riya sighed, 'Isn't he awesome?' He was. Truly.

What on earth was wrong with Riya? I thought. Most of the guys we knew were moonstruck about her and she could only see this...this specimen?

I was just about to say something blistering when Raju, the cafeteria's sole cook-cum-waiter, came cheerily up to us to take our order. We were regulars and he beamed at us with a smile as big as Lalbagh, Bengaluru's biggest garden, and displayed his dazzling yellowing teeth to great advantage. 'Saachi Madam, Riya Madam, what will you have?'

I started to say 'Coffee' but was interrupted by Riya loudly announcing, 'Dosa.' Riya was at her unpredictable best today.

'What! You only eat oats or flakes in the morning, remember? And I thought you said you wanted coffee.'

'So? People change, Saachi,' she said, nose in the air. 'And what's wrong with dosas?' she asked, warming to her theme. 'Dosas are good. They are listed at number 49 on "The World's Fifty Most Delicious" on *CNN Go*.' Riya watched a lot of this stuff, belonging as she did to a family of hoteliers. Oh well, never mind the coffee, dosas were probably in her DNA, but why the sudden change of heart? I followed Riya's eyes; her hero was stuffing himself with a masala dosa.

I ordered a filter coffee which came with foam on top and a small portion of coffee beneath. But for a Bengalurean like me, coffee is no coffee without foam on the top.

Riya was on a roll. 'I should ask Ana Aunty to make dosas more often. I'd better get used to it.' Evidently, her dreams had taken her straight to a lifetime of shared mealtimes. Ana Aunty, Riya's cook, loved her like a mother and she had practically grown up under Ana Aunty's watchful eye.

Riya was the product of an arranged marriage gone awry. Riya's mom Susie, the daughter of an NRI (or non-resident Indian for those not in the know) tycoon, had moved to Bengaluru in her early twenties to marry Riya's dad, Ray Pereira, whose family was a top name in the hotel business.

They came from very different backgrounds. Susie Aunty had lived in the US all her life until marriage, and had grown up to value freedom and independence. Her after-school hours had been spent learning to ride horses or play baseball. She would drive into the woods or go fishing with friends during her vacations. She had dated many boys during her teens.

Susie Aunty's knowledge of India was limited to visits to her grandparent's villa in Coorg. She met Ray Uncle when he visited the US on business and stayed over at her father's house, because his grandparents were close friends of Susie Aunty's grandparents.

His manners and chivalry charmed Susie Aunty. She also admired Ray Uncle's courtesy and attention to the elders. She liked the way he conducted himself during his stay—he worked hard and treated everyone with respect. Monogamy, known to be prominent amongst most Indians, was also very appealing to a girl of her age. She had seen her boyfriends break up with her when she got a pimple, or when she preferred to stay sober at parties, or something as silly as that.

When her father brought up the topic of marriage with Ray Pereira, she instantly agreed, thinking her marriage would be as happy and fulfilling as that of her parents or grandparents—

happy and long-lived. As is the way with most such things, she realized soon after she embarked on her new marital journey that all was not hunky-dory. Ray Uncle toured the world on business, while Susie Aunty had to lead a life that was acceptable to her in-laws.

There was an ocean of change in her lifestyle. She had drifted from fishing for fun to making sure that there was fresh coconut chutney every day for her in-laws. She was like a penguin which, in its need to mate, had lost its way and somehow reached a godforsaken desert. Chances of survival and adaption were bleak or almost non-existent.

Her pleas to settle abroad fell on Ray Uncle's deaf ears. The relationship suffered blows as both could not understand why a way of life that was so simple for one was so complex for the other. Peace and harmony fled the Pereira house. There were fights every day. There came a point when living under the same roof, even for the sake of their only daughter, seemed impossible. They decided to separate and Susie Aunty, her parents long since having died, relocated to the UK, where too she had friends and family. There she got so caught up in trying to figure out what to do with her life that Riya, knowingly or unknowingly, was neglected.

Anyway, getting back to Riya, I demanded to know what she meant by saying, 'I better get used to eating dosas.'

'Saachi,' she said with exasperation, 'are you always this dumb or are you pretending to be dumb? Can't you see? He likes dosas. To make a relationship work it is important to have things in common.'

'Relationship... work! Dosas! God, Riya? You haven't even spoken to him! Besides, if relationships could work by sharing dosas, we wouldn't need marriage counsellors, we'd only need more dosa counters!'

'I don't expect it to make sense to you, dodo. You are a replica of your Scooty. It has a speed limit and so do you. Anyway, after seeing him, I think I know what I want now. You just wait and watch.'

'I don't know what you want,' I retorted, 'but don't you dare comment on my Scooty. You be thankful that I let you park your Beetle in front of my house and give you a ride. If my Scooty is slow, why don't you drive your Beetle to college? That dosa boy, I mean your new flame, may notice you as well!'

Most of our fights were meaningless but we loved squabbling. What is a friendship without fights? It is like a Bengalurean turning his face from idli and sambar, a Tamilian ending a meal without eating curd-rice, a Maharashtrian breakfast without sabudana khichdi or pohe, an Andhraite eating food that's not thoroughly spiced with chillies, a Goan not eating fish for a week... I'll stop here as I am sure you pretty much get the idea.

Yet Riya was a mystery to me. When my dad bought me this second-hand Scooty I was the proudest girl in my colony. It was a luxury. But Riya had a Volkswagon Beetle, which her dad had gifted her as an expression of his love. For Riya, it simply replaced the chauffeur-driven car she had earlier used. She continued to come down to my place and go to college with me on the Scooty. Only now, instead of the chauffeur dropping her and returning, she herself would park the Beetle in front of my house, and there it would stay till we returned from college.

My parents, especially my dad, were never very happy about my friendship with Riya. Though Dad was always nice to her and would tell my mom to bring her something tasty to eat, as soon as she left he would always say, 'Stay away from these rich people.' The intentions behind his statement made complete sense from his perspective. He never wanted me to be insulted trying to befriend a rich girl. He was from a middle-class background and we had only enough to make ends meet. But I can surely say we were a happy family, with self-respect and dignity being our biggest virtues.

∽

Anyway, as of now, Riya was enjoying the dosa Raju had got, with her eyes set on her new heart-throb. Luckily, he was busy reading a newspaper and digging into his dosa. Until this auspicious moment, at least, he had not noticed her. From the bottom of my heart I didn't want him to notice her at all, ever. But I knew how hopeless that thought was.

Riya was gorgeous enough for any boy to fall for her. It would be no exaggeration to state that she got hit on by the opposite sex as frequently as I fuelled my Scooty, which gave rotten mileage. But for the life of me I couldn't believe she thought this was her Prince Charming. My gut told me that something about this dosa-boy was not right. My intuition is rarely off, and I just prayed he would disappear and she would ditch dosas and go back to her breakfast oats.

I got back to Riya, pulling her leg again, 'So why do you accompany me on my Scooty every day?'

Riya giggled, pulled my ear with affection and said, 'Because I love you, you moron!'

'And how does driving to college in your Beetle stop you from loving me?' I questioned, rubbing my ear.

Riya looked a little disturbed. I sensed that her focus was not on our mini-squabble or the dosa-boy any more. Her eyes filled with tears. 'Saachi, I have been on an endless search for love all my life. The best part of my day is when I reach your house. I love the way your parents shower their love on you.

They dote on you. You are the world to them. Until now, I am nothing but a Visa card bill to my parents. A bill that can be run up anywhere in the world and up to any amount, without my ever being asked where I spent that much money or on what, or why! Paying my bills is the end of their responsibility. I can't recollect the last time my dad and I spoke for more than five minutes. Neither can I recall any call to my mom where she listened to me, instead of talking about her globetrotting or the glamorous life she thinks she lives now.'

She fell silent for a minute. I felt helpless. She looked up, blinked back her tears, gave me a sweet smile and said, 'Tell you what! I see myself eloping with this boy on his bike and dumping my Beetle under some haunted bridge, with a note for my parents. They'll be in for a rude shock when they see I've kicked their fortune and chosen the simple life.'

The simple life! And Riya?! Every word transmitted worry signals to me at the highest possible frequency. Such thirst for love would leave her vulnerable to exploitation. I tried to drum sense into her besotted brain. 'Riya, slow down! Let's think this over calmly.' But Riya had leaped up, abandoned her dosa, and hurried away from the table, almost tripping over her chair.

I turned to see where she was heading to in such a rush and saw that dosa-boy was walking to the washbasin. Riya reached the washbasin next to his, washed her hands, turned towards him, and flaunted her expensive hair. Expensive, because Riya's salon bill usually was as good as half my dad's monthly salary.

At this point, something terrible happened according to me, and something magical according to Riya. Their eyes met!

Dosa-boy, gelled hair and all, looked frozen to the spot and Riya, sporting a thousand-watt smile, fluttered her eyelashes and blushed prettily. A regular at Page 3 parties, Riya was a well-known face. He must have realized that the dame smiling at him was the Pereira chick.

This was the last straw. I dashed to the washbasin, pulled Riya by the hand and literally pulled her away, with dosa-boy's gaze following us as we walked to the counter to pay. Even as I dragged her out, Riya had tilted her head back at an unbelievable angle to smile at him. I showed no mercy.

Riya yelled at me as soon as we got out, 'What did you do that for?'

I started, 'Riya, the dosa boy...'

'Stop it!' she said. 'He has a name.'

'And what is it?' I asked.

'We'll find out soon enough,' she said, scribbling his bike's registration number on the cafeteria bill, and then repeating it five times as if she was chanting the most auspicious mantra. 'And now,' she announced, 'I'm off to meet my fan club.'

Riya and her Romeos

෴

The fan club or Riya's Romeos, as the rest of the college called them, included seniors and juniors from the Electronics, Mechanical, Architecture, Computers and Civil courses. Riya Pereira, sole heir of the Pereira chain of hotels, was a wealthy beauty worth pursuing.

There was Sandeep whom we called the 'silent killer', because his gaze was so ardent and because he never spoke a word, though he would show up wherever she went. I guess he thought he was Kamal Haasan from the silent movie *Pushpak*. Poor fellow must have watched the movie at a very young age, because its impact on his psyche seemed irreversible.

There was Akshay the spendthrift, who insisted on buying her expensive gifts at the drop of a hat—Friendship Day, Diwali, New Year's or just a long weekend—and which she never accepted. By now, I guess he had a storeroom full of them. According to us, the best gift was the one he got her on Valentine's Day: a laminated life-sized photograph of Riya eating an ice cream on a rainy afternoon, which he had devotedly clicked.

Sagar the Facebook freak would change his profile picture every day, so that the update popped up on Riya's newsfeed and she would notice him, and so on and so forth.

But if we were to run a contest and vote the most loyal among Riya's Romeos, I would vote for Manish, who was actually also the most hard-working and good-looking of them all. Unfortunately, he was as struck as the rest of them by Riya-mania.

His day, according to rumour, began at 4:00 a.m. with studies, and every textbook had Riya's photo stuck on the inside back cover. At 7:00 a.m. he would zip on his bike from Rajajinagar to Sankey tank, a well-known lake in Bengaluru with a jogger's trail around it. Riya regularly jogged there, with her poodle Wincy, at 7:00 a.m. too—what a coincidence; not.

Manish jogged behind her at a distance, and made sure to use his well-built body to take a swipe at anyone who tried to bother her. Once Riya left, he would rush home for a shower and a quick breakfast. His next stop would be the corner of Riya's road, from where he would follow her Beetle up to my house, and from there on, follow my Scooty till college. He was such a fixture that, at one point, I almost wondered if Riya's dad had paid him to be her bodyguard.

Manish outdid himself, one day, when he made his feelings clear in front of the whole class. Earlier this year, pot-bellied Prof. Jagadeesh was egging us on to recollect Kirchoff's law, which we were supposed to have learnt the previous year. Most of the class was struggling—not to remember the law, but to keep their eyes open. The remainder was busy daydreaming.

I was occupied in picturing an imaginary conversation between a couple we had named the Adam and Eve of our class. This pair sat two rows ahead of me and were, as usual, exchanging glances as often as they could safely get away with. The conversation running through their minds probably went something like this.

Eve: I hope he likes this chiffon salwar-kameez. I spent an extra ten minutes dressing up. I am sure he loves me. He always looks so meaningfully at me. But the darling that he is, he does not know how to say it.

Adam: Wow, look at that bustline, and yesterday, her butt looked so tempting in those jeans. A deeper neckline would have been the icing on the cake.

Eve: Wow, he looks so dreamy! I guess he is imagining a romantic date with me. He is going to ask me out. Oh lord, what will I say? What will I wear for the date? God, I need to go shopping again.

Adam: Hmm, coming to think of it, if we were to run a contest of Miss Juicy Lips, Miss Biggest Boobs, Miss Fat Ass, who would be the top contenders? Oh, that reminds me, I have to shop on my way back. A new porn DVD has been released.

Our hero Manish, as usual, was busy gaping at Riya. Riya was busy sketching a pattern for her new outfit in the margins of her book. Prof. Jagadeesh happened to notice Manish's head tilted at a sixty degree angle toward Riya. To put him in a tight spot he called out, 'Manish, state Kirchoff's first law.' Manish was a bright student and this should have been a piece of cake. But instead of parroting the definition in a single breath—*Kirchoff's first law or the junction rule says: for a given junction or node in a circuit, the sum of the currents entering equals the sum of the currents leaving. This law is a statement of charge conservation*—Manish said, as if something brilliant had struck him, 'Sir, can I explain it on the board?'

Prof. Jagadeesh nodded rather reluctantly. He didn't expect Manish to know Kirchoff's first law from the second. I am sure even Prof. Jagadeesh would have 'ratta'fied, i.e., mugged by rote, this law just before coming to class.

Manish walked up to the board and wrote:

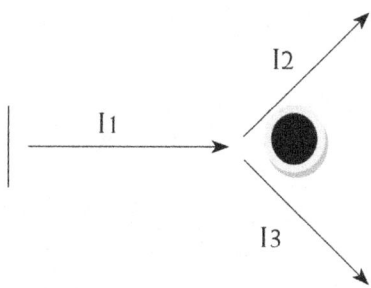

$I1 = I2 + I3$

Where $I1$ = Manish's expression of Love for Riya

$I2 + I3$ = Riya's Acceptance + Riya's Courtship

There was a loud approving roar of sound as the class rose as one to applaud the hero, and I hoped Prof. Jagadeesh would not faint, because it would be very difficult to lift a man of that size. The girls were giggling and the boys were creating a ruckus. I could sense steam making its way out of Sandeep, Akshay and Sagar's ears, boiling with defeat and kicking their asses for not having opened their mouth before Manish, in front of Riya. Their male ego was mocking them, dancing on their desks and making fun of their failure.

Riya, the focus of this entire hullabaloo that would have flustered a lesser girl, left her seat and started walking to the front of the class. I began feeling a little apprehensive. I didn't know if she would slap him or walk out of the class in rage. If she slapped him, all I could do was watch. If she walked out, of the class, my mind debated whether I should follow her out or stay put and take updates for Riya as to what happened after she left. Jesus! Friendship can be really demanding.

Surprisingly, God seemed to have heard my prayers. He saved me the stress. Typical of Riya, she did the totally unexpected. She dusted off what Manish had written and rewrote:

Where I1 = Riya's rejection of Manish's Love

I2 + I3 = Manish's Acceptance + Riya's Friendship

and she signed off with a smiley.

Prof. Jagadeesh seemed to be frozen to the ground from where I could see him. His electronic glossary, which he was banking on to make a living, had just been short-circuited. Riya stood there smiling at Manish. The professor regained his poise, tried not to look disappointed, and shook hands with Riya. After all, something is better than nothing. Then, having recovered his powers of speech, he cleared his throat and said, 'I would prefer it if the definitions were more electronic in nature.'

Clear winner Prof.! The whole class had burst out laughing and the Professor had laughed too, and then the bell had rung. Manish and Riya walked out as friends. Manish would now jog alongside Riya, not behind her. Well, they would chat more than jog, for sure. He would now meet us in college instead of us spotting him lurking at road-corners, and he could now even give Riya a lift when, for some reason, I didn't go to college.

Given Riya's usually unflappable responses, it was no wonder her reaction to dosa-boy astounded me. Thanks to her flipping out on dosa-boy, we were twenty minutes late for Prof. Sharada's class. Luckily, Prof. Sharada had stepped out to talk to another teacher over some clash in schedules, and we snuck into the class and parked ourselves in the fourth row. Manish smiled at Riya from across the class, pointed to the watch and mimed, 'Why are you late?'

Riya signalled back, oblivious to the curious heads turning to drink in the exchange. She imitated a bike, then adjusted her hair to show she was talking about a hunk, drew a heart in the air and then joined her hands and gestured, 'I need your help.'

There was an immediate change of expression on Manish's face. I could almost hear his heart break into pieces. Then he seemed to gather himself and replied to Riya's gesture. He mimed stabbing his own heart twice and pretended to faint to death on his desk!

Prof. Sharada entered, apologized for the delay, and got down to business.

Riya was restless, waiting for the class to end. My mind went back to her fascination for dosa-boy. What was it that she found so appealing that she had flipped head over heels for him? I had never seen her so dreamy. It was not that I hadn't been a witness to her numerous, spontaneous crushes. Owing to the lack of guidance from her parents, she always put her heart before her head, but so far, her crushes had been harmless. As I said earlier, I had a bad feeling about this one.

'Saachi', Riya whispered, 'I'll meet you in the cafeteria for lunch. I have work to do. I'll go out with Manish as soon as Prof. Sharada leaves. I don't want to attend the other classes.'

'Where are you off to?' I whispered back, even though I knew there was only one item on Riya's agenda. And that was finding out all about Mr Masala Dosa, and who else but Manish could help her on that.

'Where do you think, silly?' Riya looked at me like I was an idiot.

'Okay, okay!' My okay was more disagreement than agreement.

Prof. Sharada concluded her class by wishing us all the best for the internal exams which were to start on Monday.

Riya jumped up, ran to Manish, caught his hand and pulled him out of class. Her filmy exit provided the rest of us enough fodder for thought and imagination to ensure that we stayed awake over the next hour or so through class. No one can say just how good each of us students coming out of an engineering, or any other professional, college eventually proves to be in our own fields. But it goes without saying that all of us can safely make an excellent career as detectives.

Each boy, shortly after joining college, manages to get all the details about any girl right from first to final year. You name it, they have it. They can give you her name, her dad's profession, where her mom shops, the colour of her pyjamas, email ids, and her postal address down to the pin code. That is how talented our students are. They effortlessly inculcate this skill as soon as puberty kicks in. Now Manish just had to employ this skill on his own gender for Riya's sake.

Our class on wireless technology began. Prof. Somesh was of average height, wore thick glasses and looked undernourished. If all of us breathed out at the same time, he would probably get airborne and then who would teach us? He started teaching and I sat gulping water from my bottle, to better swallow the dry-as-dust complexities of wireless technology. Suddenly, an unexpected face popped around the door, looking inquiringly as if to see if this was where he ought to be—apparently it was, and the rest of him followed. It was dosa-boy.

Prof. Somesh turned to the stranger and said, 'Yes, my boy?'

'Sir, I am Vidit. I recently joined to complete my final year here, since we moved from Mysore following my father's transfer.'

Where is Riya? I thought. She should have been here!

Prof. Somesh didn't look too thrilled. He said, somewhat dryly, 'Come in, Vidit. Our head of department Prof. Menon did mention you. Your grandfather was one of the founders of the college, I gather. We usually don't take students in the final year, but as a special consideration, I suppose.'

Not that Vidit was daunted by the Professor's tone. Smirking, he sat on the chair next to mine across the aisle, and smiled as though he recognized me from earlier today. I stared back, stone-faced. If I dislike a person, it takes a lot for me to tolerate him. From the colour of his bike to the gel on his hair, the guy reeked of superficial glitter.

I decided to inform Riya. Mobiles were not encouraged on campus. We conveniently ignored this rule and slipped them into classrooms. Unlike us, they had the capability of remaining silent. I pulled out my cell and sent Riya an SMS: 'Dosa-boy in class, name Vidit. Head to base?.'

Pat came the reply: 'You must be kidding! Prepare to die if it is a lie. Returning.'

Just before I put my mobile back in, it vibrated again. Another SMS, but not from Riya. It read: 'Hey Saachi! I tuk the morn flight out. Just off the plane. Let's catch up. Lot to tell. Till then…miss u!'

Aadi was in Bengaluru. Whether she liked it or not Riya was about to take a back seat.

Aadi!

I vividly remember the day I saw Aadi for the first time, a year and a half ago. I was on my way back from our favourite hangout, Bun World. The Sadashivanagar circle signal was red. There was a fully loaded Honda CRV standing slightly ahead of me. The owner seemed to have the taste and money to support it. The CRV's handles were chrome-plated and shimmered in the street light, an elegant steel rim outlined the windows. The rear was adorned with spoilers. The tyres appeared to be 19-inches with chrome wheel covers. The modish black devil rumbled, filling the air around with rock music. I was admiring the vehicle and dreaming of owning one some day.

Like most dreams, my dream was short-lived. A hand popped out of the CRV and a well-fed, rich, so-called civilized citizen threw out an empty popcorn packet. Then he threw an empty coke tin and some used tissue onto the street. I am sure if vehicles were allowed to have feelings, like in a Hollywood flick, the CRV surely would have pushed the pedal and banged itself against a stone wall till it ended its life, for letting a pig like him on board.

I was disgusted. This is not a rare scene in India, or this was not one of the first times I saw something like this. Our day seems incomplete if we don't spot such things at some point during the day. These sightings never cease to disgust me.

I muttered inside my helmet, 'God! Teach him a lesson!' I am sure God is super busy most of the time, but there are times when He stops to listen. From the window of a bus standing next to the CRV gushed a fountain of paan juice straight onto the CRV's rear window. Bravo! It needs a lot of practice to aim and shoot so well.

I burst out laughing, but my helmet shielded my voice. All this while, I didn't know there was another spectator watching the same Great Indian Street Show. It was Aadi, as I learnt much later. He sat on an Eliminator just a foot away from my vehicle.

The CRV owner jumped out of his vehicle and started banging on the bus, calling the yokel all the names under the sun. His bad luck that the signal turned green, and as we all know, the Bengaluru Transport Service does not stop for anyone or anything, not even if God Himself stood in its way. It zoomed off, leaving the CRV owner dancing with anger in the middle of the road.

The boy on the Eliminator thoroughly enjoyed this scene. He expressed his happiness by taking off his helmet, clapping his hands and laughing his heart out. I couldn't help but notice his good looks. His hair bounced as he laughed. His laugh was irritating in a cute way, and sent ripples down my stomach. He had sexy dimples which were very inviting.

The already frustrated CRV owner stopped dancing the Shiv Tandav, and walked up to him and yelled, 'What is so funny? What are you laughing at? Do you need a taste of my hand? You crazy bugger!' The boy with the cute irritating laugh stopped laughing, put his hand on the CRV man's shoulder and said, 'Dude! You thought it was cool to litter the street, but you find it offensive when someone messes up with your CRV?'

At this, the CRV owner, who sported diamond studs in his ears, turned red, to go with the signal which had changed colours again.

He stammered, 'What…what do you mean?'

'You know what I meant, dude. Better luck next time.'

The CRV would now have thrown out all its spare parts and re-attempted another suicide, if it had not understood what the good-looker on the bike meant.

I was left with no choice but to stand and watch the drama till the end, because the CRV and the crowd that had gathered to watch the free street blockbuster were blocking my way. Even if there was a choice, I would still have waited to watch the climax.

The CRV owner seemed to give up and walked back to his vehicle. He looked as though he could not stand another minute of the unexpected stardom he had just gained as villain of the story.

The crowd dispersed, and the boy on the Eliminator put on his helmet and sped off as soon as the signal turned green. The traffic behind brought me back to my senses, honking till their own eardrums tore into a thousand pieces. All the way back home, the incident played itself out in my mind's eye, just the way a news channel would play the same footage over and over again.

I narrated this incident to Riya the next day, while we sat in her ultra luxurious room. It was redone every year to keep up with the latest interior decoration trends. If this year there was a statue of a specially made Merlion standing in a corner in her room, next year there would be an expensive Chinese vase flaunting dragons, which her dad would have picked up on one of his tours to China. Even so, Riya enjoyed shopping with me at Fab India for the simple curtains in our living-room. She never accompanied her dad on any of his tours. All she had to do was mail him some jpg images. He, by now, had developed the ability to understand what was on his daughter's mind.

Anyway, coming back to the good-looking guy I saw on the bike, Riya was ecstatic that I'd finally liked somebody.

'Babe! You were checking him out!'

'Shut up! Don't even go there!' I interrupted. 'Didn't you hear the full story?'

'Saachi, who are you bluffing? Agreed, what he did is really cool and very few boys have the balls to do that—laugh in someone's face—but admit you flipped for him.'

I knew very well such thoughts were out of my league and what was the point of dreaming about him anyway. He was really cool, but that's about it. He was some stranger I had seen on the road and I'd probably never see him again in my life.

'Okay, Riya,' I admitted, 'I was pretty impressed.' There was no point arguing with her.

This feed was sufficient for our beauty queen. Riya jumped from her bed which bounced back, considering the expensive mattress inside of it. It had given her enough momentum to land on the carpet I was lying on. She leaned over, pulled me up, put on a Sherlock Holmes look and said, 'We need to find this guy!'

'Aaah!'...I said irritated. 'Stop watching all those stupid love-struck movies.' I got up to leave. Riya walked me to the Scooty.

As I sped off I heard her saying, 'Bye, baby! You can't run too far or for too long. In the name of the Lord, I hope you bump into him soon.'

It has occurred to me many times that if Riya had not joined an engineering college, she would surely have been a Bollywood scriptwriter. The whole movie would have been about the myriad ways in which the girl-meets-boy theme plays itself out, and the name of the movie would be *Jab We Met Many Times!* Secretly though, I was hoping Riya would be right.

My thoughts were getting the better of me when I suddenly remembered the errand I had promised to run. I stopped to pick up some bread. I parked my bike in front of Baker's Nest on the lanes of Sadashivanagar, and heard a familiar laugh. My heart picked up pace as I turned to look at the man who laughed. The handsome stranger from the previous day sat there in the café adjoining the bakery, with a very pretty girl. They definitely seemed to be having a good time, while I, for no reason that I could understand, felt low.

'Ma'am, is there anything else you want me to pack?' enquired the waiter, trying to get my attention. I looked at the display. All of a sudden, it was very hard to think. I turned back and looked at the table where the couple sat. They were winding up.

Looking back at the waiter, I asked for the first thing I saw, 'Please. A pack of coconut biscuits.'

I had heard that it takes years of meditation to learn to keep your mind still. But right now, my brain felt frozen. My palms were sweaty and my mouth felt dry. I dragged myself to the counter to pay, and wondered, *God! Why are my feet so heavy all of a sudden?*

The good-looking guy walked with his hot-looking babe to the counter. He stood beside me as I was digging into my purse to find the exact change. My fingers were trembling. I could almost feel my heart thump in my ears. My eyes blurred and I could not tell the difference between fifty paise and a one rupee coin. I inhaled deeply. That made it worse, because I could now make out that I liked the cologne he'd used. He smelt like heaven. I had never before in my life found it so difficult to pull out some coins and notes from my purse.

He pulled out two hundred rupee notes and put them on the counter along with his bill. All this while, I was very clumsily struggling with a fifty rupee note and some coins. The coins slipped and clattered on the shiny counter sill. The cashier gawked at me, and evidently, I had drawn the attention of the couple. He turned to see who the culprit was. A thousand butterflies fluttered in my tummy as I realized that his gaze was fixed on me far longer than one could have expected.

I heard the hot-looking babe squeak, 'Aadi, shall we leave?' One can imagine my disappointment and my relief. Her interruption was analogous with the squeaking noise a player throws out indicating your favourite disk is damaged.

So, 'Aadi' he was. He left with the girl, who was dressed in tight jeans and a top with noodle straps. She had a tattoo of a scorpion on her nape. She had short hair and wore heels almost as tall as her.

As the scanner in my brain assessed her, I finished the job on hand, To pay! and walked out of the glass door of the bakery. I slid my purse into my sling bag. Aadi got on his bike. His girlfriend sat behind him and held his shoulders. He again turned and looked at me before he sped off. There was no way he could realize that I was the zombie with the helmet that he had seen the previous day. But yet, for some reason, he looked at me more than once.

I let out a deep sigh. As the adventure of the day came to an end, my mind was debating whether to tell Riya all about it or not. I rode the rest of the way in the direction opposite to that Aadi had taken. I was introspecting about how I had behaved earlier that evening—*Why had I behaved so strangely?*

I decided it was best not to mention it to Riya. If I did, she would start a new Bollywood story with her outdated dialogues, 'You were destined to meet him, it is God's sign to show that you both are made for each other and blah—blah—blah.'

Once I was home and in my room, I stood in front of the mirror and took a quick look at my reflection. Even though it didn't make any sense, I wanted to know if my looks were good enough to make an impact on Aadi. I was wearing a white sleeveless cotton top with a wide neck and blue jeans. I wore a gold chain round my neck with a single white stone pendant. I had a clear complexion. My hair was naturally straight and fell to my shoulders. I had bright attractive eyes. Today, they seemed to shine brighter than ever. I can't say I looked beautiful, but I could easily pass muster as a smart-looking girl.

I smiled at my image in the mirror. But the smile didn't last long. The pretty girl with Aadi appeared on my mirror right next to me and swoosh! I felt pushed down a chute. I poked my head with an admonitory finger and thought, *What is the matter with you, girl?*

After that day, much to my disappointment, I didn't see Aadi again, and he slowly receded to the back of my mind. But I should admit this was the first time I had behaved so weirdly in a boy's presence. Most times, I usually looked very serious and any boy would think twice before speaking to me. That is not to say I was not fun or did not have friends, but I was not one of those girls who could be friends with just anyone and everyone. Come to think of it, other than some movie stars, I had never really had a crush on anyone so far.

A month passed and the monsoon set in. It was a Saturday afternoon. The clouds were looking appallingly dark. I was heading off to meet Riya. We were to go to a friend's birthday party at Sigma Mall on Cunningham Road. I was just a block away from her home. I was dressed in a beige top, an ankle-length black denim skirt slit to my knees, and a pair of black sling-back heels to go with it. I hoped it wouldn't start raining before I reached her place. The thought of being stuck in rain with the thunderbolts flashing down got me nervous. I pressed the accelerator trying to get there as soon as possible.

But nonetheless, very typical of the Bengaluru monsoon, it soon started pouring. My Scooty's maximum speed of 40 km per hour was no match for the speed at which the Rain God descended on Earth. I was in a residential lane and there was no place to take cover. There were only big bungalows on the road and the street looked deserted. I had no choice but to stop. I parked my Scooty hastily and stood below a tree. Not the cleverest of things to do when it is raining, but I didn't see any choice. To make matters worse, there was a gusty wind and the road ahead was barely visible.

Should I call Riya and tell her where I was? When will the rain stop? How will I attend the party? I knew Riya would still insist I go to the party and wear one of her outfits. But how would I go home then? My dad would have come back and would not be very pleased to see me in Riya's clothes.

I thought the best choice would be to call Riya and tell her that I couldn't make it. I'd ask her to go ahead and then head back home once the rain died down. I was about to call Riya when a SUV entered the lane and slowed down near the gate of the house that I was standing in front of. The SUV stopped and the driver got down to open the gate.

A man in his mid-fifties got out from the rear of the vehicle, holding an umbrella. He walked towards me and said very gently, 'Child, why don't you come in? It's raining pretty badly.'

'No, Uncle. I am fine. I guess it will stop raining soon,' I said hesitantly. I didn't know what was uncertain—facing the fury of the Rain God or walking into the abode of a generous unknown man.

The driver had opened the gate by then and a familiar face stood there in a jacket with a hood. It was Aadi! Was I seeing what I was seeing?

He walked towards me, looked at the man and said, 'Hi Dad! You're home early.' He cast a quick glimpse at me as he spoke.

'Hi Aadi! I was a little tired, plus I thought it would be fun to watch the India–Australia match with you.'

'India finished 289/6. It's raining in Chennai as well. Play stopped by rain,' said Aadi, adding, 'I hope we catch the second innings.'

Why aren't these two men inside their spacious Land Rover or their gigantic cosy-looking house, and talking cricket over coffee? Why are they standing in the rain, on the street, in front of me? I thought. Men can talk cricket in rain, flood, draught, famine, any time!

'I got out to call this young lady inside. It is raining heavily and it is not safe for her here.'

'Yes, Dad. You are right.' He turned towards me and said, 'Please come in. I came down to call you in. I saw you from my balcony,' he said.

I didn't know what to say without sounding foolish. Both of them were being very nice to me. More importantly, it was Aadi and his dad. It was my reason to go in and a stronger reason not to go in, at the same time. 'Thanks, but I'll be fine.'

Aadi was in no mood to take no for an answer. He insisted, 'Please come in. No trouble at all!'

Well, I had to budge. He was standing there and getting wet with me for no reason.

I followed them reluctantly to a well-kept lawn. There was a hammock in the portico which led to a huge sliding door that overlooked the lawn. I walked into the elegantly furnished living-room, but hesitated to go any further as I was soaking wet. Droplets from my skirt wet the floor. I felt terribly conscious. My beige top was now sticking to my skin. I looked around as I stood with my hands folded against my chest, trying to cover most of it. There was a picture of a beautiful middle-aged woman on the wall. I guessed it was his mom. The house was colossal. I saw a helix-shaped staircase leading to the upper floor.

Aadi took off his jacket and hung it on a stand that stood near the door. He was dressed in tracks and a T-shirt which said Pepe. He called out loudly, 'Aunty.'

He turned towards me and said, 'Please sit down,' pointing to the sofa. 'I will get you a towel.'

'Get dry, Aadi,' said his dad, and waved his hand at the sofa, inviting me to sit down.

Aadi raced up as I stood and smiled at his dad. The last thing I would do was sit on the expensive looking sofa and mess it all up. Aadi returned with a towel. An elderly woman followed him. He introduced her as Ahalya Aunty, also formally introduced me to his dad, Mr Rajeev Murthy. Ahalya Aunty, as I gathered later, was Mr Murthy's widowed sister and had no children. I could instantly sense the deep bond between Aadi and her.

Despite the elders in the room and despite being drenched and feeling awkward, my mind was turning cartwheels. I noticed Aadi's gorgeous face had tiny droplets all over. He had a stubble and looked better than ever. His dimples deepened every time he smiled. He had inherited his mother's dimples and her eyes. He handed the towel to me and said, 'I think you know my name by now. I am Aadi and you are...?'

'Saachi,' I replied. 'I was going to my friend Riya's house. Riya Pereira,' I added. Everyone knew the Pereira family, especially when they lived just a block away.

'Ah...yes!' he nodded and so did his dad.

'I know Ray Pereira quite well,' his dad added.

His aunty said, 'Saachi...Nice name. Please sit down. I will make some hot coffee for all of you.' She ruffled Aadi's damp hair affectionately as she walked out.

Aadi's dad looked like a perfect father figure. He was in his mid-fifties, athletic looking, had real dense dark hair for his age, a tall nose and kind eyes. I noticed a few dark lines below his eyes indicating he was tired. He now excused himself and went in to change, but stopped midway and turning around, admonished Aadi, 'Make sure this child does not step out in the rain, Aadi,' and turning to me, said, very kindly, 'Make yourself comfortable child.'

We were alone in the living-room. I had to act quickly or, surely, I would end up doing something stupid. I looked around. There were steps at the corner of the hall. I walked up and sat on them. I commended myself for the great job I had done so far.

Aadi smiled. 'I think the sofa will be more comfortable,' he said, pointing to the plush cream coloured sofa with grey designer cushions and pillows. 'I am fine here,' I said smiling, wiping the water off my hair and half covering my shirt with the towel.

For a minute Aadi seemed lost. I could see his eyes run over my hair. Riya always teased me that I looked my sexiest in wet hair. His look was affirming that. I had goose bumps all over. I had to keep calm. I was in his house. I could hear the coffee cups clinking in the kitchen and did my best to divert my attention. I had to keep my focus. As impossible as it seemed at the moment, I had to do my best not to be intimidated in this Greek god's presence.

'I have seen you before,' Aadi said. I stopped wiping my hair for a second. My heart raced again.

'At Baker's Nest,' he continued. I could not believe my ears. So did he really remember me? From the sixty seconds he had seen me on that day? Why did he remember me? Was it because I was clumsy or was it something else?

I had to reply. *What would be an intelligent reply? Should I tell him that I had seen him twice before, or should I say, 'Oh Really?' and look innocent. Riya was correct. I scored two on ten in this area.* My thoughts raced.

I chose to be upfront. 'I have seen you twice before,' I smiled. 'I saw you the day before I saw you at Baker's Nest, as well. At the signal...the CRV man...the paan-spitting fellow from the bus.?'

Aadi burst out laughing. 'Oh yeah! That day I was uncontrollable. It served that pig right! So were you there?'

I nodded, 'Yes! I was parked right beside you,' *and was almost hypnotized,* my mind reminded me. Ahalya Aunty chose that opportune moment to make her entrance with coffee and potato wafers. She sat on a chair close by. For the next few minutes she chatted about how unpredictable the weather was in Bengaluru. She also warned me to stay safe on the roads especially on a two-wheeler. She spoke about the zillion potholes, the loose electric wires, the feeble-rooted trees, etc. On a lighter note she narrated how Aadi enjoyed walking back home in the rain as a schoolkid, rather than come home by car.

Before I could get to know more, the phone rang in the adjacent hall. She excused herself and went to take the call. She was a friendly person and I noticed good looks ran in their family.

Where is his mom? Had she gone out? I wondered.

Aadi came up to my perch on the stairs and stood leaning against the wall beside the stairs. His proximity was making it a little difficult for me to breathe normally. He sipped his coffee and so did I. The coffee tasted just perfect. It was the best coffee I had ever had. Maybe I was exaggerating. Maybe it was not just the taste but the fact that I was having coffee with Aadi. That was what made it so special.

There was silence in the room. As I sipped my coffee my mind went back to Baker's Nest and the coffee suddenly tasted bitter.

Aadi was looking at me, 'Are you alright?'

I cursed my expressive face. 'Yeah, yeah...I am fine. I was enjoying the coffee. It tastes awesome.'

Aadi relaxed and began conversing. He wanted to know where I studied, what was my subject, how I knew Riya, where I stayed, etc., etc. I spoke to him briefly about my mom Gauri and dad Shankar. I told him my mom was a homemaker and dad worked as a teller at a bank.

It was my turn to question him. I learnt that he had completed his B Tech, and in a few months was to join Symbiosis in Pune for a MBA program. His dad owned Murthy Exports, Murthy Granites and Murthy Furniture, and managed all three almost single-handedly.

Then the topic moved to a more sensitive subject. Hesitantly, he spoke about his mom. He said her name was Jeeva. Aadi had lost his mom four years ago in an accident, and from what I could see, he missed her terribly. He fell silent all of a sudden.

'That's her in the picture,' he said with a half-smile.

I was caught off-guard. I felt uncomfortable and didn't know what to say. I could not even imagine a life without my mother. This was the first time I was talking to him. I didn't know how much was too much! All of a sudden the sound of the rain lashing down furiously sounded very loud in the room. It seemed to fill the space between us. I had to say something. I wanted to bring that captivating smile back on his lips. But I also knew, no matter what I said, nothing would change.

I really didn't know what to say, and blurted out, 'You have a very good bike.'

That is what came out of my mouth, but my heart wanted to do something entirely different. I wanted to walk up to him, hug him, and run my hands in his hair.

Aadi smiled. He said, 'Yes, I think it's great. In fact, I am crazy about bikes.' Aadi comfortably switched to the topic of bikes. He seemed as enthusiastic as a kid and spoke of his bike tours and a recent road trip he had taken. He also told me that at some point he wanted to tour India on his bike. He was looking for company to do that, I gathered.

'Ah! Good,' I said. 'You have a very pretty girlfriend, I'm sure she'd enjoy going for the trip.'

Aadi's eyes flew wide open. He looked confused and said, 'My girlfriend! Really? How does she look? I mean, who is my girlfriend?'

I wanted the earth to open up and devour me. Whatever little impression I must have made so far would have been definitely damaged by my stupid statement.

Quick, Saachi! I told myself. *Damage control. Use your grey cells. Say something!*

'I am sorry,' I said, giving him an apologetic smile. He could see in my eyes that I meant what I said. 'It is too personal. I should not have brought it up.'

'No, no. That's alright! What's there to mind? I don't have a girlfriend.'

My heart leaped in excitement. I hoped I wasn't grinning like an idiot. It was the happiest moment of my life by far. But of course, I did a good job of holding back my excitement. I looked surprised and said, 'Sorry again. I saw you with a pretty girl that day in the café. I think I got it all wrong.'

'Oh! Sarah! No, no…she is my friend. I met up with her as she was leaving for Mumbai to meet her boyfriend's parents. Things are going well for her. I think she will get married soon.'

Wow! Could anything get better? God bless me, God bless Aadi and God bless Sarah and her boyfriend and his parents. I was exhilarated. The door to courtship was wide open!

'I don't think I will ever have a girlfriend,' he said.

One moment I was soaring and the next I came crashing down.

What was he saying? Why did he not want a girlfriend? He was handsome, kind at heart, intelligent, rich; he had everything he wanted. Why not a girlfriend? Did he mean he would go in for an arranged marriage? God! Or worse. Was he gay? Oh no? What a royal waste!

He continued, 'I don't believe in relationships. I don't believe in marriage.'

'Oh! Okay! Good,' I said, sounding as less disappointed as I could. At least, he was not gay.

'You think that is good?' he questioned. He must have found me weird. I was cursing myself for getting into this conversation.

'I mean, you must have your own good reasons for it. There is nothing right or wrong about it.' I said.

'Hmm. Yeah,' he said, and I could sense something running at the back of his mind.

I started as my cellphone rang. It was Riya. I said, 'Excuse me,' to Aadi and picked up the call.

Riya was hysterical on the other end. I should have called her, but had lost track of time as soon as I saw Aadi.

'Where the hell are you? Why aren't you here?' she screamed.

The last thing I wanted to do was tell her where I was. For all I know she would drive down to Aadi's place and wax eloquent on my behalf? But I could not lie in front of Aadi. What would he think of me?

'I got stuck in the rain. I cannot make it,' is all I said.

'What do you mean, I cannot make it? You know I will not go without you,' Riya screamed again.

'Riya, I am sorry. This was unexpected.' I did not want to tell her that I was just a block away from her place.

Riya banged down the phone. She had lost her cool. I let it be for the time being as there was nothing I could do.

I was hoping the rain would stop soon and I could head out. I had stayed in Aadi's place for quite enough time.

'Looks like Riya likes you a lot,' Aadi grinned as he said that.

'Ha ha,' I muttered. I explained as briefly as I could and then realized it had also stopped raining. Getting up, I thanked Aadi and requested him to thank his aunty and dad on my behalf as well.

'Thanks for all your help. If not for your dad and you, I would have ended up with a fever tomorrow. Bye!'

Aadi followed me, and all of a sudden, seemed very dejected. 'Did you leave anything behind?' he asked.

I quickly checked. I had my sling bag, my keys and my cell. I smiled and said, 'No, nothing!' As cheesy as it sounds I was leaving my heart behind. I knew it didn't make sense but not everything was under my control.

He walked out of the gate with me. He didn't have to do that.

I got on my Scooty and got ready to leave. I looked at him for a minute. He was smiling again, and to my shock, he said, 'Saachi, has anyone told you that you have beautiful eyes?'

I didn't know what to say. My eyes popped out. I was clearly blushing. This was unexpected. He had made it clear he was not looking for a girlfriend. Then what was the flirting all about? Like they say, change is the only constant! Maybe something inside him was changing. I decided to play along.

'Yes! My boyfriend tells me that all the time,' I smiled. *Boyfriend! When did I get one?*

'Oh! Okay,' It was his turn to look disappointed. There was no reason for him to be disappointed, but for sure, he was.

'You didn't tell me you had a boyfriend,' he said.

'You didn't ask,' I laughed.

'Yeah, right!' He sounded a little pissed off. He put his head down as he spoke and scuffed the wet mud with the toe of his slipper.

I decided to stop. 'I was joking,' I said, looking at him.

He lifted his head instantly. 'A bad one,' he retorted. So there was another side to his jovial and easy-going self.

'Maybe,' I smiled, and started my vehicle. 'Bye again,' I said. 'Bye!' he mumbled.

I had moved just ten yards when I heard him call out, 'Saachi!' I stopped. *What was it?* I turned and looked at him.

'I didn't take your number. Maybe we should meet again.'

'Sure!' I gave him my number. So there was something on his mind too. But you never know, I thought. I just wanted to let it flow and not have any preconceived notions.

I stored his number as well. It sat first in my contacts—Aadi.

From that day on Aadi called me every day. Strangely, it felt like we had known each other for a very long time. We met every second day whenever we had even a second to spare. All other plans would go out of the window if we had to meet. We spoke about anything and everything. We became very good friends and we were both extremely comfortable with each other. Baker's Nest was our favourite hangout. I started to get to know Aadi better, every passing day.

Finally, the day came when Aadi had to leave for his MBA course at Symbiosis in Pune. He had told his dad not to come to drop him off at the airport. He said he was not comfortable. But he wanted me to be there. It was time for him to check in.

He looked restless. There was a lump in my throat but I didn't want to cry in front of him. I maintained my poise and said, 'You must leave now. You will be late. Study well. Have fun and take care of your health.'

He looked into my eyes. Till date I am not sure that what he did after that was an expression of what he felt, or if he understood my absolute yearning. He took a step towards me, dropped his bags, put his hands on my shoulder and said, 'Saachi! Have I told you? You are my best friend. I will miss you terribly. I have never come so close to anyone, all my life. You make me feel very good. I enjoy the time we spend together. You take care while I am not here. I will come down at every chance I get. I don't know what I will do without you around.'

I could not hold back my tears any more. He pulled me close and held me tight in his arms and kissed my head. A teardrop fell on my shoulder indicating he was crying too.

I wept like a baby in his arms. The warmth from his body was comforting. Being in his arms felt like a safe haven. I could not express myself as freely as him, but my tugging at his collar and hiding my face in his jacket said it all.

Aadi kept his promise for the last one year he had been in Pune. He called me more often than when he was in Bengaluru. Distance didn't matter. He would come down to Bengaluru for the silliest of reasons, and spend most of his time with me while he was here.

Riya was damn excited about Aadi's entry into my life. No matter how many times I told her that we were just friends, she stuck to what she felt. She always said that we had great chemistry. But she had promised me that she would not mention any of that to Aadi, and not be a drama queen when he was around.

Catfight

෴

Dreamily thinking of Aadi, I came back to earth with a jolt when Prof. Somesh thumped his hand on the table to make a point. He was doing his best to make his class on wireless technology as gripping as possible. Carrying on about the 'wireless family', he informed a half-asleep class of the first generation of wireless transmitters that went on air in the early twentieth century, using radiotelegraphy—Morse Code. He then added that the TV, fax, cellphones, GPS, GPRS, cordless phones, cordless mouse, etc., were all children and grandchildren of the same technology.

Bright student that I was, I easily converted our theory class to a practical one. I had put these electromagnetic waves to best use by transmitting an SMS to Riya, on Vidit's arrival in our class, to my revulsion.

Riya raced up the stairs with Manish by her side as soon as she saw my SMS. Her sprint time would have put the service providers to shame, because their speed of SMS delivery seemed like ages in front of her lightning connectivity.

She stood at the classroom door panting, as though her dash had a noble cause behind it, like the Bengaluru Marathon, with an agenda to save the city's greenery. Gosh! If she had not run at that speed, Bengaluru would not have looked green any more!

Manish stood beside her. To my fancy it seemed like Manish was destined to either jog beside Riya or run up the stairs with her. We know boys run behind girls, but I think it is just a phrase. Manish is the only guy I know who has actually done justice to it.

Riya expected to find Prof. Jagadeesh in the class. The Professor had a soft corner for this beauty and Riya made full use of this fact. Now she looked slightly confused to see Prof. Somesh on the dais.

Nonetheless, even if she had walked in to encounter a two-headed Tyrannosaurus gaping at her, she would still have made her way in. Now since it was harmless Prof. Somesh, Riya simply said, 'Excuse us, Sir!' and marched in. Her eyes quickly spotted Vidit who sat looking, along with the whole class, at Riya and her partner. Looking at his amused face I felt as uncomfortable as a canine that senses earthquake tremors much ahead of its owner. Danger was lurking at close quarters.

'Where have you been? Why are you so late?' Prof. Somesh tried to sound as authoritative as possible with his meek voice, which matched his weak body very well.

Manish looked helplessly at Riya's face. I don't think he had an answer that could cover the couple's absence.

Luckily for him Riya came to the rescue. Anyway, it is a proven theory that men usually melt when girls come up with excuses. Their undefeated belief for ages has been that girls don't lie! Even if they do, there must be a very genuine, unutterable reason behind it!

'Sir, we had been to the library to get some books that we wanted to look up for some extra reference for Monday's internals,' Riya gave him the first excuse that occurred to her.

Little did Prof. Somesh know that Riya was oblivious about the college library's location, let alone its Reference section or even if it had one. She was Riya Pereira. Even if she wanted to look up extra references, all she had to do was make a phone call. The library was for people like us who could not afford all the books in the market.

'Hmm…where are the books then?' the Professor asked sceptically.

It was Manish's turn to rescue Riya. He replied before Riya spat out one more lie and got caught.

'Sir, on the way it struck us that they don't issue books on Friday, and so we rushed back to class,' replied Manish.

Riya, wide-eyed, looked at Manish. She must have realized her inexperience with library schedules. Manish nodded knowingly at her.

I giggled. Vidit looked at me. I turned away. *Brute! I don't like you. To top it, I don't like my friend being cross-questioned like a criminal because of you,* I thought to myself.

'Hmm. Okay! Come in,' Prof. Somesh seemed convinced, and must have felt very happy to have such hardworking students under him. Manish definitely had credibility being among the toppers in college.

Prof. Somesh continued his dive into the wireless world. Riya joined me at my desk, and with a flick of an eyebrow sent Manish to sit next to Vidit. Riya shook hands with me under the table. I was her partner in crime!

I heard Manish whisper, 'Hi! I am Manish and you are?'

'Vidit.' They shook hands. For the rest of the class, Manish spoke in a hushed voice. He tried to collect a complete database of info about Vidit. It was so detailed that he could put it up as a Wikipedia link. Riya was sitting beside me, but her ears seemed to have developed the power of picking up low-frequency sonic waves that the rest of us could not hear. 'Riya,' I hissed. 'Sshhhh,' she signalled. It was no use talking to her now.

My mind was painting horror movies on a white washed wall. I feared that Riya was just five minutes away from an intro to Vidit. I could picture the scene. Prof. Somesh would leave as soon as the recess bell buzzed. Everyone would walk out for lunch. Manish would continue to converse with Vidit in order to hold him back in the class until Riya walked up to them and was introduced. I would make my way out of the class as I had made up my mind not to be around. I was not ready to witness the disaster. Riya would then ask Manish, *'Shall we go for lunch?'*

'Yeah, Riya! Sure! By the way, Vidit, do you want to join us for lunch'?

That would have been enough for Riya to take her imagination to the point where she would decide where to honeymoon with Vidit.

As my thoughts galloped, the bells screeched to give the time for students to feed their growling tummies and get set to doze off in the second half.

Prof. Somesh prepared to leave as he gathered his notes. Some students were already out before him. Riya was adjusting her hair and checking if her pastel coloured dupatta was in place.

She gave me a questioning look.

'You look ravishing,' I promptly replied.

Prof. Somesh stopped near the entrance as he was walking out, as if something struck him. He turned back and said, 'Manish, Riya, please come with me.'

Both their faces turned pale with this unexpected call. The same thoughts were running in all our minds. *Was he smart enough to know that they were lying earlier? If he did come to know, what would he do? Would he take them to the HOD's chamber and reprimand them? Or would they get away with a casual warning? What was there to stress so much? It is not the first lie he would have heard or the first time someone came late to class.*

The Professor continued, 'I am very happy to know that you both take your studies seriously. So what if they don't issue books to students on Friday? They do so for professors throughout the week. I will get you whatever book you want in my name. Please come with me.'

I was dying to laugh. The look on Riya's face was worth a million bucks.

'No sir... That is fine... Why the trouble?... We will manage,' both Riya and Manish spoke alternately to complete the sentence.

'No trouble at all! It is my pleasure.' The Professor seemed pleased with himself at his generosity.

There was no way out. 'Thanks a lot, Sir!' Manish said, and walked behind the Professor. He did not want any more complications.

In the meanwhile, Vidit had walked out of the class. Riya started banging her fist on the desk.

'This is how lucky I am,' she said.

'Relax, Riya! He is not going anywhere. You have all the time in the world,' I pacified.

'Please wait for me in the cafeteria,' she said, as she followed the Professor and Manish. She had to do that as she wouldn't find the library otherwise!

I thought hard as I climbed down from the third floor and made my way to the cafeteria. *How do I make Riya slow down? We should go easy on this. How much do we know of Vidit? Is Riya really ready for this? Is Vidit the right guy? Am I being paranoid?*

❧

My mind partly blamed the vacuum in her life that her parents had created. All she got from them was a caretaker and loads of phone numbers to reach anyone she wanted. From her designer to her doctor, everyone would assist her on the phone or drop by, but her mom rarely came to visit. When she did, her dad made sure to be out of town. If they crossed paths by mistake, there would be a fight, which Riya would overhear sitting on her plush bed holding Wincy in her arms. He would show his concern by whining every time a teardrop fell on him.

As for the conversations her mom had with Riya when she came down—'Riya! What is that hanging on your body? Do they call that a dress? You look so bad in these local designer dresses. They don't show your body line too well. There is no oomph factor. Why don't you fly down to London? My friend owns a boutique in Paris. She has everything that is new in fashion.'

She would then ruffle her hair. 'What's with your hair? Have you checked out your cousin Rinky's new look? She is any designer's pride. Mrs Sharma has invited me for a party. I want you to accompany me and meet some boys and get a life. But before that, we need to find new clothes for you. Let's choose the best of the worst we find here. We need to hurry up. I want to take you to the salon with me, to set your look straight, before I leave.'

Riya would cry her heart out every time her mom left. Not because she left. It's only because she had not changed even a teeny-weeny bit from her last visit. She would always hope that her mom would change some day, and behave like a mom and not an agent who was prepping her up to take part in the Miss World contest.

Riya, by now, was used to making all her decisions on her own, and was not really used to caring what others actually thought. According to her, those who knew her well enough, like me and Manish, would not misunderstand her.

How accurate can one be in decision making when one has no one to look up to? I can't blame her, I thought, as I entered the cafeteria.

There was nothing much I could do other than sit there and wait for Riya and Manish. I took a corner table facing the window. From where I sat I could see anyone coming into the cafeteria. I sat looking into nowhere and hoping the duo would turn up soon.

'Can I join you?' I heard a voice. I lifted my head to see Vidit standing there with a plate in hand.

No way! my mind resisted. I would die of indigestion if I ate with him.

'Actually, no!' I said rather bluntly. I am usually not rude to people; then there are times when I am quite happy about my curt behaviour, like these.

'I am waiting for my friends to join me. We will run short of chairs,' I said. *And you are not welcome. Buzz off, you rodent,* my mind completed the conversation.

If Riya got the slightest hint that I had driven Vidit away, it would be the end of our friendship. I peeked out of the window to make sure she was nowhere near the cafeteria.

'Oh, that's not a problem. Here...' said Vidit, dragging another chair from the adjacent table. 'Is it okay now?' he smiled.

How shameless can someone get! There were other boys from our class in the same cafeteria. Why couldn't he go sit with them?

He reintroduced himself again, 'I am Vidit.'

'I know,' I said, looking at my mobile. I was not expecting a call but I didn't know where else to look.

'So you are not having lunch?' he enquired as he dug into his plate and chewed his food noisily.

'I am waiting for my friends, like I told you before,' I replied.

'Hmm. Tell me, what does the crowd do here on weekends?'

'There are lots of things you can do. But I take magic classes.'
It was a true lie.

'Wow! That is cool! So can you show me some magic?' he
smirked.

'I am actually thinking of making you vanish into thin air
with my magic,' I said. I was making it very obvious that I did
not like his company.

He laughed. God! What a devilish laugh! Half the cafeteria
turned to look at us.

'You're very interesting,' he said.

It is irritating when you don't mean to talk rudely or crack
a joke, and people misunderstand you. It is even more irritating
when you are intentionally rude, and people think you are joking
and take it easy!

*You shameless ass! I would have buried myself alive if someone had been
so snappy at me,* I thought.

As I sat in front of my uninvited guest, doing my study on
how tricky conversations can get, I saw Riya racing towards the
cafeteria with four books in her hand. It was one of the rarest
sights.

As she entered our den, much to her pleasant surprise, she
saw me sitting there with Vidit. Her eyes grew bigger in size.
She put her thumbs up and gave me a big smile. I guess I had
proved that I am her best friend and it meant I had done a good
job. I thought so too, as it was the longest I have tolerated
someone I dislike, and if not for Riya, the scene would have
been different.

Vidit noticed me looking at someone behind him and he
turned to see who it was.

Riya immediately put her hands down and tried to look
very casual.

Manish tried to take the chair next to Vidit. Riya pushed him and indicated he should sit beside me, and she sat down next to Vidit.

'Hi Vidit,' said Manish, 'I see you've already met Saachi. Meet my friend Riya.' No time wasted, I see. I felt bad for Manish. He was being a good Samaritan but driving nails through his own foot.

'Oh! So you are Saachi. I didn't know her name,' Vidit replied, ignoring Riya.

Attitude! I thought. Riya's face looked small. She was not used to being ignored. All her life she had been the centre of attention! This was new.

'I must say, Manish, your friend Saachi is not only good-looking but a very interesting person. She has a good sense of humour,' Vidit said, giving me a rather amused smile.

I got up abruptly. I had never felt so uncomfortable before. I hated the game this stranger was playing. I pulled Manish and said, 'Riya, wait here. We will go get lunch. What would you like to eat?'

Riya picked up the cue. She looked at Vidit's plate and asked him, 'How does the biryani taste today?'

He said, 'Good,' and continued to eat without even looking at her.

'Okay, I will have one,' she said. Manish and I left hoping they could get some privacy and Riya could strike up her much desired conversation.

'There is something wrong with that guy,' I told Manish, as I stood in the queue to pay and collect the food coupon.

'Why?' Manish asked.

'Why? What do you mean why? Can't you see? He rides a yellow bike, has gelled hair, laughs like a devil and did not notice Riya!'

'Saachi! What is it with you and yellow bikes and gelled hair? Boys think it is cool and we like to believe that even girls think. Yellow bikes are a rage these days. I think you are overreacting.'

What he said was irrelevant to me. I snapped again, 'It's no use jogging by her side every day. Do you need so long to win her heart? How can you give up so easily? Couldn't you turn friendship to love?'

Manish was a stud, very sharp in studies and a very good friend, and moreover, he was ready to do anything for Riya. Many girls had shown interest in him, as we were aware. But he was attracted to Riya. I personally preferred to see them pairing up. I knew Manish would keep her happy.

'Saachi, relax!' Manish spoke as he took a deep breath. 'What do you expect from me? Agreed, I like Riya, but you have to understand, I am not obsessed with her. Let's face it, she doesn't feel the same for me. We both know I tried a lot initially and was very disappointed when she rejected me. But at the end of the day, I am glad she is my friend.'

He took a step ahead as the queue moved on and sighed, 'I agree, I am a little partial to her, but I am a friend to her just like I am a friend to you. Moreover, I always wanted to be her partner, not her poodle!' he replied as he paid for all three of us and bought biryani plates for everyone.

Wow! There was more to Manish than I thought. Manish making such mature statements irritated me all the more. Every sigh of his also indicated that he was not too happy either, but at the same time, he would not thrust himself on her.

Why is Riya not attracted to him? It is hard to find such sensible guys who can be as crazy as him to try so many ways to impress a girl, but at the same time take rejection so gracefully. That shows his confidence. How many boys can accept rejection? They won't rest till they prove that the girl was a slut, just because she couldn't be theirs. They even forget it was the same slut they were ready to do anything for.

We walked towards the table with biryani plates in our hands.

I saw that both of them sat silently at the table. No matter how much I hated it, we had to help them converse. The day was becoming very stressful.

'So are they very strict about internals here? In my previous college the questions were shared, so that all of us would score well and the college had more pass percentages. All we had to worry about was the finals,' Vidit said, looking at me.

What is wrong with this guy? I thought. *Why is he doing this? Why he is talking only to me?*

I deliberately didn't reply. I acted like I didn't hear the question. I continued his game.

Riya seemed to have lost the power to speak. There was silence at the table. It was unusual to see Riya so silent. She usually spoke at least five sentences, fifty words each, in thirty seconds! Okay! I am exaggerating a little.

Manish had to reply. He shifted restlessly in his chair before he said, 'No. We get assessed quite strictly here. In fact, our internals are tougher than the finals. They do that hoping we are well prepared for the finals.'

'Who tops the class?' Vidit asked.

'Saachi, of course,' Manish replied promptly.

'There has been a time when you topped as well,' I reminded Manish, squirming at this unwanted attention.

'That was only once. It's been you all the other times,' Manish asserted.

'Hmm, intelligent and modest,' Vidit sounded impressed. 'You don't look studious.'

How do studious girls look? Is there a type? Should they be plump, wear fat glasses, come to college with coconut oiled, plaited hair, and eat in classrooms and not in the cafeteria as they prefer the aura of classrooms? What is this moron's intention? I thought. Whatever it was, it was not going well with Riya, as I could see.

'Where are you putting up, Saachi?' he continued questioning.

Riya's face was red by now. I was boiling inside. *What the hell? Where is this going? Why does he care where I stay?*

'Why do you want to know?' I couldn't hold it in anymore. Even for Riya I couldn't pretend to be nice.

'I stay in Sheshadripuram. So I was wondering, if you stayed anywhere close by, we could meet up and I could use some help from the topper,' he replied.

'I always study with Riya at her place. She lives in Sadashivanagar. You can come there,' I replied, without mentioning where I stayed. It was my last hope to make it up to Riya. I could ask him to come to her place and then make an excuse of not being able to get to her place, so they both could study together.

'Hmm. I am not sure,' he said.

Riya got up at this point. 'Sorry,' she said in freezing tones, 'I have to leave.' She took her half-finished biryani, dumped it in the bin, and stalked out in anger.

I ran behind Riya, without bothering about my plate or excusing myself. Manish would take care of the plate and Vidit as well. I hoped he would pour the gravy from my plate on Vidit's head.

'Riya, stop. Where are you going?' I was panting for breath as I followed her.

'Go away, Saachi,' she yelled, without turning. She was walking swiftly towards the main gate.

'What happened? Why did you leave? Where are you going? Wait!' I yelled back. I had seen enough drama for a day.

She stopped, turned and looked into my eyes. I had never seen her so angry before. She was short-tempered but she would watch her temper with me, and at times, I would tolerate it, as there were many good things about her.

'You really want to know what is wrong?' Riya said, fuming. I was confused. As far as I knew I hadn't done any wrong.

'Yes, why are you so angry?' I was confused.

'You...' she started. 'You know what, let it be. Let us not talk.' She turned her back again and started walking.

I caught up with her. 'No, wait. Let us go together. What is it that you don't want to talk about? Out with it. I am your friend, remember?'

'Don't call yourself that,' she yelled, 'I think you have always been jealous of all the attention I get.'

Now that was a bummer. I stepped back. She continued irrationally, 'Wait, let's see. No! I don't remember anyone asking you out so far. I have always been the hot topic in college, and somewhere, I think, this has affected you and you were waiting for this chance.'

She closed her mouth with her hand as if to hold back from crying, 'But why Saachi? Why him? Not after you know that I like him.'

Again, her voice rose. She dug her eyes into me and screamed, 'What did you tell him before I came that he is so entranced by everything you say and completely ignores me? What were you doing at his table and what did you bitch about me?' Riya was insane with anger.

That was it. I lost my cool as well. 'Stop it, Riya! Have you gone mad? Can't you think straight? He joined me at my table and I had no role to play in that.' I rubbed my forehead.

'By the way, do you want to know what I think of that joker? I think he is a major put-off and not a match in any sense, and definitely not my type of guy. If I have been tolerating him, it's only for your sake.' My hands and body spoke more than me.

I moved restlessly in my place, shifting my weight from my left leg to the right. 'Trust me, you are making a big mistake— one, by being interested in him, and two, by fighting with me for that complete stranger!'

It hurt. It hurt badly. I couldn't believe my ears. This was not Riya. Not the Riya I had known for the last four years. What the heck!

'Not your type of guy? Huh! Really! So you have been considering him even after you knew what I felt? It's hard to hide the truth, isn't it?' Riya was almost in tears by now. She held her head with both her hands.

Damn it! I couldn't cry. I was too angry to cry.

'Have you lost it, Riya?' I said. 'Is that the only sentence you heard come out of my mouth? Why is that you understand only the things you want to understand? How in God's name should I make you understand?' I expressed my genuine concern.

I was tired of screaming by now. I saw Riya's lips tremble as well. I felt bad and decided to gain control.

I moved towards her. I held her hand, pushed her hair behind her ears, put my hand on her cheek. 'Please calm down. You know it is not true. Let's talk this out.'

For a moment she seemed to calm down. She knew in her heart that I was telling the truth. It was more to do with her being ignored rather than thinking that I was stealing the show.

But it was like something horrific dawned on her, and she pulled away. 'Do you think I am a fool? You think I don't understand? It is my fault to have trusted you so blindly. What is the problem with you middle-class girls? Why can't you tolerate other's happiness? Don't ever talk to me again. This is over.' And with that she stomped off, her back rigid with righteous indignation.

I wanted to slap her and bring her back to her senses. But my ego was like an injured soldier by now. I was no more in a mood to convince her. I didn't want to indulge in cheap talk about her or her background and pick on her weaknesses. I just wanted to go from there. I was choking, ready to cry any minute.

I ran to where my vehicle was parked. My phone rang. Aadi's name flashed on my screen as I reached my Scooty. I picked up the call reluctantly. I was breathing hard trying to hold back my tears.

'Hello!' I heard Aadi's voice and burst out crying.

Aadi was shocked, 'Saachi? Are you crying? What happened? Why are you crying?'

I sobbed uncontrollably, hiding my face in my palm for the next two minutes. Luckily, there was no one in the parking lot.

'Saachi, please stop crying. Say something,' Aadi begged.

'Please let me cry. Don't ask me any questions. I am in no state to talk,' I spoke in my broken voice, between sobs and wiping my tears which were not ready to stop.

I could hear Aadi start his bike.

'Stay there. I am coming,' he said. Before I could utter another word he had cut the call. Any further calls to stop him from coming were not answered.

Aadi to the Rescue

❧

Having failed to reach Aadi again, I sat on my Scooty balancing it with both my legs. For the first five minutes my tears and emotions refused to subside.

An unpleasant trailer of what happened a few minutes back played out in front of my eyes. Whoever the writer was, the script was quite depressing. *What the heck just happened? What was she talking about? What made her think I would fool around with that jackass? Why the middle-class crap? How do my dad's earnings decide how good or bad I am?* The more I thought the more depressing it was.

Aadi called again, 'Saachi, where are you? I am at the entrance.'

'Parr...kinggg...' my voice was hazy. Why is it that we become weaker when we know there is someone around who cares for us? *I have Aadi to talk it out with. What will that stupid Riya do?* I felt sick in my stomach when I thought of her.

I heard Aadi's engine die down behind me. He walked up to the front of my Scooty.

'Wow! You look beautiful,' said Aadi, pulling my leg. My kajal was all over my face, my eyes were swollen. I looked like a wreck as I could see in my small front mirror. I had wet at least five tissues by now.

'Shut up!' I punched his arm. 'You think I am a joke?' I got off the Scooty.

'No, I think you look beautiful even when you cry,' Aadi's voice softened. He had to bend to match my height. He stood leaning over, bending his knees slightly. He wiped my face. He caressed my cheeks with the back of his fingers like I was a baby.

He put his hand on my shoulders and walked me to the banyan tree close to the parking. We sat on the slab there. He took my palm and squeezed it gently.

'Now tell me, what happened? Why is Mademoiselle upset? For the sake of the world, please stop crying. Save paper, save the earth,' he cooed.

I let out a small laugh. I didn't like crying very much and how long can one cry?

'Riya,' I said.

'What about her?'

I filled him up on the disastrous episode of the suspected love triangle and the catfight that was responsible for my current state.

'She is plain stupid. Why do you even have to cry over that?' He looked surprised.

'Aadi, it is Riya I am talking about. You know how close we both are and how much I like her. We know each other for a long time now. It bothers me that she thinks this way about me.'

'Hmm. So what do you want to do now?' he asked.

'I don't know. I want to kick his ass; he is responsible for all this,' I replied through gritted teeth.

'Okay, done. Apart from that what do you want to do,' he smiled.

I replied with silence. To be frank I didn't know.

Aadi took a deep breath and chewed over the possibilities. 'Aah!' he said and jumped up, 'I can help if you want to make up with Riya.'

I looked at him with one eyebrow raised and my face read, *How?*

'Okay, here is the deal. There is a party tonight at Mr Sharma's residence. It is my friend Nitin's birthday bash. By the way, that is something I have been waiting to talk to you about. I want you to accompany me to the party.'

'Why?' I asked. 'Why should I come? I am not even invited.' I was reluctant.

'Hey! The invite goes out to me and my partner, and I'll take you along. There is a special reason behind it. Sharma Uncle wanted to gift Nitin a bike. But not any old bike out of a showroom. He asked me if I could get it modified. Then me, Mr Genius, stepped in and...well, I don't want to beat my own drum. Why don't you come and check it out? I have designed it.' He sounded excited. 'I want you to tell me what you think of it.'

'And why does what I think matter to you?' I asked.

'Saachi,' his voice was now impatient. 'You very well know how much I like you. But if there is anything at all that I don't like about you, it is the number of questions you ask. Why are girls so fond of asking countless questions?'

'Because you dumb boys never come straight to the point.' I was not used to giving up easily.

'What do you mean?' Aadi asked.

'Ha ha. Why are you asking a question now?' I giggled.

'You either ask questions or answer with giggles. It is so tough to converse with girls,' he said.

'I know,' I replied, 'It is tough to match up to our IQ.'

'Don't even get there,' he said. 'Anyway, your IQ is driving us away from the actual issue. Very typical! Girls can never stay on one topic,' he added, pulling my leg.

'Go to hell! I am not coming anywhere. Neither do I want to make up with anyone.' I jumped off the slab as I said this and started walking towards my vehicle.

'Oops, sorry!' Aadi caught hold of my hand and stopped me. 'I plead guilty, I irritated you. I think I should spare you today.'

It was tough for me to be angry with Aadi for long. I obviously gave in.

'So how can you patch me up with Riya if I come to that party?' I asked, coming to the topic I was more concerned about.

'Nitin is a common friend of ours and the Pereira's. I am hoping Riya will be there.'

It started making sense now.

'Even if she doesn't happen to come, I still want you to come there with me, for the reasons that I just told you,' he added.

I liked anything and everything Aadi did. I knew his passion for bikes. I wanted to accompany him as well.

'But do they allow middle-class people there?' I asked

Aadi's face changed in anger. I could hear him clench his teeth. I had never seen this look on Aadi's face before.

'Next time you say that, I will slap you.' He said. 'The rich are also born human. We are made of emotions too, we also laugh, we also cry. I would rather judge a person by his or her attitude and not by their bank balance or the bungalows they own. How nice you can be at heart is how rich you can be. By the way, let me reiterate to you, you goose, I am as penniless as you are and still live on my dad's income.'

I watched agape. I didn't know what to say. What Aadi said made sense. *Just because Riya was immature, it didn't mean I had to be like her. Who am I to judge people?* I thought.

'I am sorry. Point taken,' I said, furtively trying to whisper into his ears.

'You better be,' Aadi said, as he pulled me towards him again.

Aadi followed me to my place and asked me to be ready by 7:00 p.m. He said he would pick me up from home.

My mom noticed my swollen eyes as I entered the house. On being questioned I made up a story saying I had hurt my eyes. Mom just remarked, 'I hope you are alright.' I was happy that my mom was not the nagging kind.

I had skipped the afternoon class. A good nap would do justice to my absence in the class.

Aadi was at our house that evening at 7:00 p.m. sharp. He walked into the kitchen and asked my mom very sweetly to make coffee for him. He had got a pack of my mom's favourite Bhakarwadi and Amrakhand from Chitale Bandhu at Deccan, in Pune. He had just upgraded her weekend menu from sleeper class to first class AC coach! She thanked Aadi.

My dad was out on his evening walk.

Aadi called out as he walked out of the kitchen, 'Aunty, I visited Sarasbaug. I have put in your offerings and prayed intensely to give Saachi some sense. I also took a darshan in the Laxmi temple across the street. You were right. It is beautiful.'

My mom called back, 'I told you.' My mom had visited Pune with her friends when they had been to Shirdi to visit the famous Sai Baba temple-shrine.

Mom came out in five minutes, placed a tray with Bhakarwadi and coffee, and told Aadi, 'Join us for breakfast tomorrow. I will make puri to go with the Amrakhand.'

Wow! I thought. This mango-flavoured variety of Srikhand was my favourite. I loved its sweet and tangy taste.

'Sure. I will be there,' Aadi was more than ready.

I wore a sleeveless white frock with a boat neck for the evening. I added a small pearl necklace and pearl earrings, while Aadi was busy talking of his holy darshan and food with my mom. I wore white slingbacks to match my dress and put on light make-up. I wore my hair pretty.

There was a reason I was wearing that dress. Riya had gifted it to me on my birthday and it would be a good start to make up with her, and white meant peace!

Aadi kept smiling without any reason every time he looked at me. It was more of an 'I am totally hitting on you' kind of a smile.

He was dressed in a grey shirt and dark blue jeans. His hair was bouncy as usual, and his broad shoulders and small waist made him look breathtaking. As ever, he smelt sexy.

My mom went in to her hideout, the kitchen, to start on her preparations for dinner.

I threw my clutch at a non-vigilant Aadi.

It hit his forehead. 'What did you do that for?' he said smiling, looking at me in a way that made me feel pretty self-conscious, 'You really look stunning,' he said and added with a wicked grin, 'which is so unlike you.'

'What! Just say that again!'

'Nothing, chipmunk. Just kidding.'

'Yeah, sure, fatso,' I said as I called out to tell my mom that we were leaving.

Fatso! Aadi was terribly conscious about his body. He was a fitness freak and I knew how to irritate him.

'Fatso?' he reconfirmed.

'Yes, fatso,' I replied as I got onto his bike.

We carried on pulling each other's leg as we rode to Nitin's house. There was no winner. That is what I liked most about being with Aadi. Most of what we spoke was meaningless, nonsensical stuff, yet made so much sense to us. We liked to make each other laugh. After all, there is nothing much you gain by being serious all the time. I knew that most of Aadi's friends who happened to be girls were ravishing and stylish. I was no match for them. But how many of them could he connect to, relate to and converse with for hours, as he did with me?

Mr Sharma hosted the bash on the brilliantly lit sprawling lawns of his house. I could see the younger lot having a good time on the first-floor balcony, which was big enough to accommodate at least twenty guests. Loud music played in the background. I wished they would turn it down a notch.

Strangely, the swimming pool area on the far side of the lawn was unusually dark. That didn't go well with me. I thought some lighting there would have made the party look more inviting. That apart, the party was just perfect.

We were received at the porch by Nitin and his dad. Aadi introduced me as his friend. I caught Mr Sharma wink at Aadi. Aadi responded with a smile.

'Where is the bike?' I asked Aadi, as we walked into the lawn. My eyes were simultaneously searching for Riya.

'That's a secret. You have to wait until all the guests arrive,' Aadi replied.

I spotted Riya as we spoke. She stood there in a corner, talking to a group of friends. I saw Manish with her.

Riya didn't notice me. She was beautiful in a black top and black trousers. Her fair skin was visible through the lacy top, which highlighted her perfect shoulders. The colour she wore was the opposite of what I wore. Maybe it depicted her mood as well. She wore a diamond neckpiece which glittered in the dark night.

As I walked towards the seating area, to my shock, I saw Vidit at the bar counter.

Aadi asked, 'What happened? Why are you looking so shocked?'

'Vidit,' I replied, and pointed to where he was standing. 'There, at the bar, in that shiny red tight top,' I said, disgusted.

I am sure he thought he was a stud but he looked like junk to me. He was a fashion disaster.

'Stay here,' Aadi said, pulling a chair for me. 'Try not to be seen. I'll be back soon.'

'Where are you...?' But Aadi was gone before I could finish my sentence.

I saw him head to the counter. He asked for a drink and got into a conversation with Vidit, effortlessly, within a matter of minutes. Both of them were looking at Riya from where I could see. They seemed to be having a good time. I hoped Aadi knew what he was doing. The last thing I wanted him to do was make friends with Vidit.

He stood there at the bar for the next ten minutes. By now, Riya had spotted Aadi standing with Vidit. She didn't seem too happy about it. But I am sure she didn't suspect I would be there at the party, or even if she did, she showed no signs of looking for me.

Aadi left the counter and walked to the other side of the building and vanished. I was still trying to make out where he had gone when my phone rang. It was Aadi.

'Saachi. Try to sneak out from there. Take the first right from where you are sitting. Walk around twenty steps and you will see a coffee table. I am there. Come quickly.'

I was curious. I felt like a super sleuth from a hit detective series as I walked past the crowd, following Aadi's directions. All I was missing was a gun tucked somewhere in the folds of my dress.

Luckily, neither Riya, Manish or Vidit noticed me. I met Aadi at the coffee table.

'What is all this? Why did you call me here?' I asked in curiosity.

'Relax. You were right about Vidit, Saachi. He is a jerk. His intentions are hideous. He apparently has been using reverse psychology to get Riya's attention. He is definitely not serious about her.' Aadi looked around and checked to make sure that neither Riya nor Vidit could spot us.

'He plans to get her into bed the first chance he gets, and to dump her when he gets bored.'

'That sick bastard! How did you get all this out of him? I mean, you were gone just ten minutes!'

'Simple,' said Aadi, 'I just stooped to his level and began commenting on Riya. He instantly opened up; plus he is already down with four drinks. Free booze,' Aadi explained.

'Yuck! So you too pass comments on women!' I pulled a face.

'Is that important now?' Aadi was angry. I was undermining his efforts.

I decided to move on. Aadi was right. This was not the time to focus on Vidit's vulgarity.

'Okay, but how did he land up here?' This question had been bothering me right from the minute I had seen him at the party. I was not sure if I could make up with Riya with that clown around.

'He's here because of your stupid friend Riya. She asked Manish to bring Vidit along. Any idiot can see through her ploy. In fact, Vidit called her easy bait. She's walking into his trap more easily than he expected. He doesn't even have to try.' Aadi looked slightly worried.

'I want his real face exposed,' I said furiously.

Aadi nodded; we were quiet for a minute or two, trying to think of how to show Riya Vidit's true intentions. Suddenly, Aadi's face lit up. 'I got it!' he said with a grin, and before I could ask him anything more, he zipped off telling me to 'Enjoy the party!' and asking me to wait at the same table as before.

He was nice enough to send a waiter to my table to give me a drink and some starters. I didn't know what Aadi was up to. And I had no choice but to sit and wait. He walked away with a grace that was so natural to him.

I could see Riya and Vidit exchanging glances and an occasional smile, mostly from Riya, from where I sat. Vidit was sending her just enough encouraging signals—after all, she was easy bait, as he had told Aadi. The crook definitely knew the tricks of the trade.

I looked at my watch; at least ten minutes had passed since Aadi had left. He was nowhere to be seen. I looked at the bar; Vidit was tossing back drink after drink, while a waiter silently began clearing the bar counter. I watched as the poor man neared Vidit and stumbled over a stool, spilling a drink all over that red shirt and Vidit's trousers too.

Enraged, Vidit got up, his fist ready to punch the helpless waiter until he realized Riya was looking at him. Not wanting to spoil the great impression that he was intent on making, he unclenched his fist and dropped his upraised hand. The waiter, meanwhile, was apologizing over and over again and finally convinced Vidit to go with him. Vidit turned and smiled at Riya as he walked with his arm around the waiter's shoulder, probably because he could no longer walk straight after all that drinking. They walked to the pool's changing area, and I cast my eye around. I saw that most of the guests had arrived, and finally, so did Aadi. He quickly grabbed some snacks from my plate and said, 'Come with me.' There was no time for questions.

We moved towards the pool area. He made me hide within hearing distance of the changing rooms. I could see the waiter standing outside in the dim light. Vidit was inside. It had been an eventful evening so far.

Aadi whispered that he had bribed the waiter to spill the drink on Vidit and take him to the changing rooms.

Vidit had now pushed a hand out of the door to give his shirt and trousers to the waiter to dry, and was yelling, safe in the knowledge that Riya was out of earshot.

'You dog! You messed up my evening. If not for you I would have been dancing with that girl there in a few more minutes. Idiot! Get these pressed. If you don't get back in five minutes, I'll drown you in the pool.'

I heard the waiter apologize, 'Sorry, Sir. I will press it and get it back to you in a jiffy.'

'Where is he going?' I whispered. Aadi stood behind me holding my arms. Even in that hubbub I could feel his warm breath on my neck.

'Sshhh. Just watch,' he said.

'Doesn't he watch Bollywood movies? Is he an idiot to give away his clothes?'

'When you are drunk,' said Aadi, 'you can't really think. You should get drunk some day.'

'Very funny!'

Aadi laughed and told me to stay quiet and wait till he returned. Then he walked back to the lawn again.

I stood there for the next ten minutes. Nothing happened. I was kind of losing my patience. The waiter didn't get back. I think even Vidit lost his patience. He first peeked out of the changing room. He looked around. The area was dark. He was looking at something. My gaze shifted as well. In the dim light I could see a satin cloth spread on something. I could not make out what though. Strangely, it was hanging above the pool.

How on earth did it get there? I wondered. Vidit started walking towards it. He had to get something to cover himself. Maybe the mosquitoes were eating him up.

He slowly walked up to the satin spread. I could hear him walk on something, probably a wooden plank. If not for his foot tapping on the wood in the dark, it looked like he was walking on water! What on earth was a plank doing there! Vidit was intent on the satin cover for his shorts.

Where was Aadi? Vidit's slow walk over the plank would be over soon. Suddenly, a terrific noise rent the air with dazzling flashes of light—a fireworks display! The fireworks caught the attention of the guests. Within seconds the whole pool was brightly lit.

I could now see what I couldn't see in the dark. Vidit was, to his shock, standing on a dais and the satin was spread on a bike. To make things worse, a trolley supporting the dais now moved it to the centre of the pool before Vidit could make up his mind to jump ashore. Vidit was caught like a rat in a trap, and was looking around frantically, wondering how to get out of this mess.

'Ohh,' went the crowd. They probably didn't know how to react either.

It looked like Nitin's dad had spent a bomb to make it all so adventurous for him. The spectators were getting their money's worth.

The dais was stationary now and Vidit leaned over to dive into the pool. We heard a motor kickoff and the dais began revolving and rising vertically. Vidit lost balance and fell on the dais.

'Ooooooh,' went the crowd.

A spotlight shone on the bike and on Vidit as well. He wore shiny underwear with the moon and stars on it.

A Bollywood number, 'Dhoom machale, dhoom machale, dhoom', blared from the speakers.

Riya was looking at him, appalled and ready to faint. Vidit lay there like a frozen statue, unsure of whether to stand up or whether he was better off lying down. He had involuntarily gone around twice on the dais by now. He finally gathered his wits and pulled the satin spread off to cover himself.

The audience cheered wildly. He was part of the show and a fabulous-looking bike had been revealed. High entertainment indeed.

Nitin and his dad wore uncertain looks—Nitin, because he knew nothing about all of this including the bike, until it was unveiled—and Mr Sharma because he knew about the bike but not about the scantily clad male who was wrestling with the satin sheet and rolling on the dais. He turned to Aadi questioningly, and Aadi promptly signalled the dais operator to bring the dais back to the edge of the pool. Thereupon, Vidit, the satin cloak draped around him, fled like a bat out of hell and vanished— probably in search of his clothes—and was not seen again.

Someone passed a mike to Mr Sharma who cheerfully wished his son a happy birthday and added, 'May life surprise you always and I pray you live it to the fullest. I want to thank Aadi, who is also like a son to me, for the efforts he took to make this bike look like a mean machine. You are truly talented, son.' Aadi responded with a gentle nod.

Nitin spoke next, 'Thanks, Dad. I love you. Thanks, Aadi. You rock! Dude, you made me happy. To all the lovely girls here, I hope you enjoyed the stripper. He seemed rather shy though. Dad, haven't we paid him? Girls, we can call him back if you didn't get a good look at him.' Nitin's father laughed loudly and clapped. The guests followed suit.

I joined Aadi and we shared a laugh. Aadi had indeed done a great job on the bike. Nitin rode it round the pool with his dad riding pillion. He was thrilled. Mr Sharma thanked Aadi again in person. We danced into the night. Riya later left the party with Manish running behind her as usual. She didn't realize I was there at all.

A Wish Comes True!

Though I had been unable to get Riya to patch up, Aadi and I had done a good job of messing up Vidit's plans of getting anywhere close to Riya.

I was up early on Saturday morning to finish studying so that I could meet Aadi for lunch, without feeling guilty.

We drove seventy kilometres down Mysore road on Aadi's bike and stopped at Kamat Lokaruchi, the restaurant styled with a *Malgudi Days* ambience and known for its jowar roti thaali. The waiter poured lots of ghee on the roti while we sat laughing, talking over the previous evening's events. I was visiting this place for the first time. The waiters in their typical Karnataka style wore a dhoti with a shirt, and a small shawl on their shoulders. It added a rustic feel to the place.

'So you didn't tell me what you think of the bike I designed?' said Aadi, as I sat admiring the place.

'Hey! I didn't know you were so good at it. Liking bikes and designing them are two different things. I must say you did a good job on it. I was impressed.' I showed my genuine appreciation.

'Nice. What did you really like about it?'

'Well, er...' I paused. Then, with whatever little knowledge I had on the subject, I gave my judgement.

'Your design made the bike look sleeker, the stickers you chose for the extra front guards looked good, the handle modification made the bike look sporty.'

I cleared my throat and continued, 'I saw that the regular tyres were replaced by bigger ones that made the bike look sturdy. I don't really know if you did something to enhance the performance of the bike. Honestly, I wouldn't know the difference. But it looked sexy.'

I felt very proud of my little speech and that I knew so much about the mean machine. I expected Aadi to be pretty impressed about it.

Instead, he said, 'God, you are an illiterate. You don't know anything about bikes, do you?' He laughed.

I was offended. 'You are mean. You want to know what I know of bikes. Okay! I know a bike has an accelerator which men find convenient to vent their anger with, a horn which boys consider below their dignity to use, lights which blind others, a silencer which most of you guys don't think is necessary, brakes which you don't use till the last minute, an indicator which will become non-existent in Bengaluru very soon as no one uses it, mud flaps which are never cleaned, two wheels which bear your weight and that of anybody you carry pillion. I know enough of guys and bikes. What else do you want me to know and with whatever knowledge I have, I think I described the bike you had worked on well enough.'

'And now,' I said, 'Let's see what you know about jewellery.'

'Oh, that's easy,' Aadi sounded confident. He opened his palm to display his five fingers, 'Diamonds are a girl's best friend.' He folded one finger. 'Gold is a father's nightmare and then the husband's.' He folded another finger. 'It comes in all shapes, sizes and designs.' He folded another finger. I promptly opened it back and said, 'That does not count.'

'Okay, okay. Here's the best one… It is the only way to a woman's heart and often to her bedroom.' He folded his third finger and pulled back his hand so that I couldn't reach it to unfold any other finger.

'The bigger the diamond, the happier and more forthcoming the lady.' He folded the fourth finger.

'Not to forget, good food for the next one month', Now his hand was a fist with all five fingers folded. He pulled up his collar proudly as he came to the end of his description.

'You are so gross, Aadi. Eew.' I kicked his leg under the table.

'Hey! That's not fair,' he grinned.

'Just because girls don't talk dirty, it doesn't mean you can get away with whatever you say.'

'Talk dirty, baby! I like it,' he pretend-growled.

'Shut up!' I scowled as he grinned some more. We ate in peaceable silence.

'Riya doesn't have to go through this,' I said to Aadi.

'Agreed,' he replied. 'But there is only so much you can do.' He had a point.

'Let me try to call her,' I said.

'Go ahead if you want to. But I don't think you should. Yesterday's episode would have upset Riya all the more. Assuming she still has doubts about you, I suggest you leave her alone for a while.' He had made a point again.

I fell silent as I thought of Riya. Everything would be different if we continued like this. There would be no more fun and frolic. Going to college would be such a pain. I heaved a deep sigh.

'Saachi,' Aadi said, trying to divert my attention, 'do you want to hear about my trip to Sinhagad last weekend?'

'Yep. What does Sinhagad mean? Any idea?' I was curious.

'Sinh for lion, and gadh for fort,' Aadi explained to me. 'It's perched atop a hill at about 800 metres and was named after Tanaji Malusare, one of Shivaji Maharaj's great generals, who laid down his life in a battle fought there.'

'Wow. Interesting!' I was impressed.

'You know what is more interesting?' His eyes shone. He continued, 'It is said that Tanaji scaled this steep hill with the help of a monitor lizard named Yashwanti, locally known as a ghorpad!'

'A monitor lizard! It had a name? He managed to climb a hill with its help?' History and its heroes never ceased to astound me.

'Yep. Tanaji and his troops captured the fort, but Tanaji laid down his life in battle. Grief-stricken, Shivaji said, "We conquered the fort but lost a lion." So that is how the fort got its name.'

He went on to describe how beautiful the hillock was during the monsoon. He described the mist, the rain, the greenery; the hot bhuttas, kanda bhaji and pitla bhakri that they ate; and all about the trek.

'Wow, you seemed to have had a good time,' I said.

'Yes! It was fun. I even made some new friends who had tagged along with my friend Sid,' he said. 'I particularly liked a girl I met, Mahi. She was so cool. She is a very nice girl and I must say pretty adventurous too. In fact, she was the one who made me aware of the history of the place. I was quite impressed. She says she has trekked many hillocks in and around Pune, right from her childhood. I like such girls who don't spend the summer sleeping on a couch.' Aadi was excited about his new-found friend. He even showed me her picture captured on his mobile.

Everything had gone so well so far. Suddenly, my eyes began burning and I rubbed them.

'Hey! Are you alright, Saachi?' Aadi held my hand as if to stop me from causing any further damage to them.

'Yeah! I slept late after the party and got up early to study. I'll just go and splash some water on them,' I said and excused myself from the table. As I walked to the washbasin, I saw a girl walk by with a quote on the back of her T-shirt that read, 'If you like someone, let him go; if he comes back to you, he is yours, otherwise, he never was.'

Wow! Signs! I thought.

I very well knew all the while that there was nothing I could complain about. He had made it very clear to me that he was not interested in a relationship with me or any other girl. That didn't stop me from feeling what I felt, and at the same time, I didn't expect any reciprocation. I wanted to cherish what we had, and what we shared was a very special bond.

I walked back to the table.

I spoke of Riya again. 'She thinks she loves him,' I repeated what I had already told Aadi before.

'Yes, you have told me. But love? Don't you think love is a very overrated word in the world of hooking up or dating?' he said.

I gave him a look which said, 'Go on.'

'What is that phrase? Love at first sight!' He looked bewildered as if it were an alien concept.

'Whoa! Whoa!' I said. 'Aadi, just because you are indifferent to this topic, it does not mean everyone feels the same way.'

'I don't expect anyone to think that way! It is my opinion. Has it ever occurred to you, in one look, how do you know you love the person? I can agree if someone says I like the way a person looks, or her mannerisms, the way she dresses, her eyes, or her smile, or whatever. I can understand being attracted to someone and wanting to know more about the person. But love?' He was sticking to his point. 'Why can't people date for a while and then decide whether they want to take it to the next level or not?'

'Like Westerners do?' I asked.

'Yeah, what's wrong? Doesn't it make sense? For me, it is very important to know the person before I commit,' he said. 'I cannot simply commit to someone I met at a discotheque, in a mall or at a party, at first or even second sight. It is about my life and hers as well. I'd rather date her and then decide how to take it ahead.'

'Aadi, do you think it works that way here in India? Here in some regions, marriages till date are decided without the boy and the girl seeing each other before marriage. Then there are families who are a step ahead, where the girl and the guy get to see each other in front of a dozen relatives.' I looked around. There were enough travellers around, couples actually who sat at the same table and ate, but looked at each other like complete strangers.

I sighed and moved on, 'The women from both sides will discuss and compare the lavish marriages that they recently attended and the men will talk on current affairs, like it is the apt place to do so. Then they sign a business deal as to how much each party will get or lose in that marriage.' It was my chance to show frustration on the topic.

'We still live in times where a girl has to pay a lifetime maintenance fee to get married, and a boy has to prove he is not impotent if he does not demand dowry,' I ended.

'Exactly,' replied Aadi, 'So don't you think it is time to change some of these things? Is marriage a pact? A compromise?

Don't you need to be in love with a person to get married? Can I marry a girl for what comes with her? How many parents understand what chemistry means?' He pushed the tissue holder on the table.

'You seem to be writing some kind of a thesis on this,' I pulled his leg. 'Why are we even discussing this? This is a never-ending social issue. Anyway, you don't believe in relationships, so no question of love.'

Aadi's face fell all of a sudden. I had unwittingly trodden on a tender spot. I felt horrible for doing it, but it was too late. It was done.

'That is a different story,' he said. He sipped some water, looking nowhere.

I was in an awkward situation. I didn't know how to get back after derailing the conversation.

'Come to think of it, there is only one true love at first sight,' he said very gently. His voice was very tender and his eyes were moist.

I touched his hand across the table. I slightly caressed it. He needed comfort. I didn't know what he was thinking. But whatever it was, it hurt him real bad. May be a failed love story, I thought. I didn't have to ask him what he meant because he did start talking about it.

'When a mom sees her baby for the first time, holds it in her arms, touches her cheek to the baby's and kisses its forehead—that is love at first sight to me. Even if you are the ugliest baby ever, she still finds you beautiful and loves you unconditionally all her life.'

A teardrop wet the table cloth. So there was something amiss. I figured that it had something to do with his mom. But I would not want to know any further till the day he was comfortable talking about it.

Aadi was a fun-loving person to the outside world. I am not sure how many of his friends or family knew about what a softy he was at heart. I was moved by the way he described love and the bond between a mother and a child. For sure, losing his mom was a big blow to him.

They say, *A son can outgrow his mother's lap, but never her heart.* I guess it is the same with a son too. No matter how old he is, how independent and strong he thinks he is, a mother will always have a special place in his heart.

'Aadi, what you say makes sense,' I said softly. 'I am sorry for dragging this conversation in the wrong direction. Please don't feel bad. Besides,' I added briskly, 'you look quite horrible this way.'

'Ha ha,' laughed Aadi. 'I will kill you if you tell anyone that you saw me crying,' he said. 'By the way, in spite of all that I have said so far, there was one incident where I experienced love at first sight!' He gave a naughty grin.

They say a woman's heart is a deep ocean and no one knows how many secrets are hidden in there. But let me tell you, boys give good competition too. You never know what they are hiding from you. I wondered what it was now.

'I fell in love with my bike the moment I saw it. I brought it home with love and we've been inseparable ever since,' he said.

'Very funny,' I said. I was glad that our conversation which had turned unexpectedly serious ended on a funny note.

We drove back home. I said bye and went up, and I guess I dozed off even before Aadi had walked out of our front door. I slept like a log for the next two hours. I woke up early in the evening and studied. That night when my mom called me for dinner, I still felt heavy from the afternoon lunch. I decided to take a walk on my terrace.

I had grown up in this ancestral house. We had a spacious lawn, a portico supported by pillars, teak doors, opening to a living-room. It was a three-bedroom house. The doors creaked every time they opened or closed indicating they were ageing. My mom had decorated every corner to jell with the slightly ancient architecture.

There were jute hangings and mats. There were ethnic lampshades and beautiful copper diyas. There were her own hand-painted vases. Every door had indoor plants on either side. The sofa fabric was sober, bringing out the ethnic hues. The curtains were carefully chosen. There were desks, corner tables and a rocking chair, all made of rosewood that had been handed on from generation to generation. The living-room had a door at its one end which led to the terrace verandah.

Well, right now, the verandah opened to a view of concrete jungle outside. I recollected my days a decade before, when I would sit on the terrace and look at the stars and bright moon at a time Bengaluru was not over-populated as it was now. Well, old or new, the city ran in my blood. I sat on our three-seater swing with my eyes closed and enjoyed the cool evening breeze. Then I got up and took a walk, looking at the coconut trees that had grown in our compound.

Aadi left for Pune on Sunday. He promised to come back in a fortnight. I had to hold the fort on my own, on Riya's front, till he returned.

He gave me some advice before he left. 'I know your intentions are good, Saachi, and how much you care for your friend, or any of us. But never forget, you too are important and don't let anyone walk all over you.'

That evening I felt awfully lonely and didn't feel like studying in my room. I sat in the hall and skimmed through my notes, revising for the second time. Riya dominated my thoughts.

My mom kept looking at me from across the hall where she sat knitting. My dad sat in his rocking chair and read his favourite R.K. Narayan book. All his friends went to play cards and drink in clubs, but my dad enjoyed spending time with his family at home.

My mom broke the silence. 'Saachi, is everything alright?' she asked.

I was brought back to this world. 'Yes, Mom,' I said. The most difficult thing is lying to your mom.

'Where is Riya? She didn't come down to study yesterday; neither did you go to her place.' She was looking for an answer.

I put my eyes down. I didn't want to answer this question, at least not when my dad was around. 'Weren't you saying that you were interested in yoga classes,' I asked Mom. 'Shall we walk up to the instructor's place? I have the address. It is a ten-minute walk from here. If you like what he says, then you can start from tomorrow,' I said.

My mom was quick to understand. She was my best friend and talking to her about anything in this world was very easy, and she would always help me see my problems with greater clarity. What would this world be without moms? If I could be half as good as her in my life, I would consider it well-lived.

As we walked to the instructor's place, I narrated the whole story to my mom.

'She is not to be blamed, Saachi. You know her upbringing has many pitfalls. She has no emotional support. By the way, what you did at the party is the best part so far. It serves him right. Don't worry. Sooner or later, she has to realize it. Just be calm till then. Don't take what she says too seriously.'

I felt much better now. I had my mom and Aadi on my side. Riya had no one but Wincy to talk to, who did a very good job listening, by the way!

To my surprise Manish called me later that night at 9:00 p.m. He sounded low.

'What happened?' I asked.

'Riya has lost it,' he said. 'That buffoon Vidit embarrassed everyone at a party yesterday.'

'Yes, Manish. Aadi told me what happened.' I avoided telling him that I was there.

'So how is Riya now?' I asked.

'I told you, she's lost it. She was pissed with me for what happened. She felt it was my fault.' He was angry.

'What! How was it your fault?' I was concerned.

'She thinks she can use me as she wants. She has no respect whatsoever for me. First, she wanted me to get him along to the party. Next, she wanted me to stick around with him all the time. Is he a toddler? She thinks if I was with him all the time and not with a new group of friends I made, all this would not have happened.' He was frustrated.

'She also said that you and I have let her down,' he concluded.

'Forget it, Manish. You know what she is saying is sheer nonsense. It had to happen some day. If not Vidit, then with someone else. But I know for a fact his intentions are not good. Let's think of how to get her out of this.'

The next day I went to college all by myself. It felt strange Riya not talking non-stop or banging on my helmet. I saw her Beetle parked in the campus. It was attracting attention. There was a change in Riya.

I entered the classroom where my register number was allotted for our internals. Manish was already there. The test was to start in ten minutes. I could not see Riya. Vidit would have been allocated a seat in another room as alphabetically he would come last.

Riya came into the class five minutes later, didn't look at anyone and sat down. Prof. Sharada was the invigilator. She handed out the Blue Books in which we wrote all our internals, and gave us the question paper. We had sixty minutes to finish. It was graded for twenty-five marks.

Every semester, we had to appear for three internal tests for all subjects. The best of two would be considered for the average score, and that would be added to the final exam score.

This was our first internal in the seventh semester. I wanted to make sure I scored high in the first two, so that I could take the third internal with ease.

Riya was clearly struggling to finish her paper. She was distracted and she must have spent the whole weekend on the phone with her new-found boyfriend. She scribbled as much as possible and left in a hurry, fifteen minutes before the final bell.

I was done with the paper as well. I raced behind Riya as she handed over the paper and stepped out of the class.

'Riya,' I called from behind. But she did not bother to turn.

I caught hold of her hand and said, 'Riya,' again.

She stopped, turned and yelled, 'Let go off me, you bitch!'

'What the hell, Riya? What is the matter with you? Have you totally lost it? He is taking you for one big ride. Please don't fall for that, and don't you dare call me by that name again,' I slammed back.

'I didn't ask for your gyan, grandma. It is none of your business. Stay clear. If I want to screw my life, I will. Why should it bother you and how shameless can you get, talking to me even after you know what I think of you? For your own good, don't let my tongue lash you again.' She was fuming. It felt like she was possessed by a devil.

By then Vidit had come out of his class and had heard our last conversation.

'Shall we make a move, Riya?' Vidit asked, as if he was unaware of what was happening.

You wretched rascal, I thought in my mind.

They walked ahead while I stood there not knowing what to do. As they passed Vidit turned back, pursed his lips, blew a kiss my way and winked.

I didn't hesitate to mock him, taking off my heel and pointing it at him. I didn't realize Manish came from behind. He had seen what Vidit did. Vidit must have felt like a winner breaking the bond between Riya, me and Manish. He had no hurdles now. Plus he had a beautiful, rich idiot to rejoice with.

'Saachi, we have better ways to deal with that asshole. Don't stoop to his level. We have to act smart. We can't prove to Riya what he does behind her back. She is blind, deaf and dumb now. Whatever we say will fall on deaf ears and she will spit shit. Forget it.'

I was happy with how well Manish handled it, unlike other boys who can get real sissy at times. If not that, they react violently, end up stalking the girl or threatening her with false allegations or foul-mouth her.

Riya, Manish and I were quite outspoken in our conversations. We usually had our conversations in coffee bars. While Manish would get many of his questions about women's 'mysterious' behaviour answered by us, Riya and I did our own research on male psychology. There was a lot Manish knew about Riya's private side that he could have taken advantage of. But he was a gentleman and never abused his friendship.

'I am going to give him a taste of his own medicine. Manish, let's follow them. Who cares what they think? I don't want to leave him in peace.'

'Where to?' asked Manish.

'Wherever they go!' I was already running down the stairs and my foot briefly touched every alternate step.

I was putting my sneakers to their best use.

'You think it is a good idea?' Manish asked, in between breaths.

'I don't think it is a bad idea.' I had stopped breathing! At least, it felt that way.

We decided to take Manish's bike. We could come back to get my bike later. We saw the blue Beetle take a turn at the gate. We overtook the car that was driven by Vidit. We made sure we were in clear view of the driver. At a signal Manish parked his bike to the side and asked me to swap seats, with him riding pillion. Riya and I always wanted to give it a try but he had never approved. Now I gladly agreed and I wore his helmet. My hair flowing below my shoulders gave my sporty look a finishing touch.

Even though we were not very comfortable with the objective of the joyride, we forced ourselves to look naturally in high spirits.

There were times when Riya and I were on my bike and Manish was on his beside us, and we raced each other. Riya would scream 'Faster, Saachi. Faster!' We hung out all the time and went to movies, bowling and played badminton together at Riya's club. Aadi would accompany us whenever he was in town. Riya would tease Aadi, 'Hi Aadi, as in half,' and Aadi would reply, 'No, it is Aadi, as in first.' Those were good times when our friend was still sane.

They drove about twenty kilometres towards the outskirts. At a junction the road merged into a highway. They chose to take it. I rode confidently through the highway as I had observed the traffic thinning down due to the hour of the day. They definitely were not enjoying the drive. Every time they overtook us I could see that Vidit was trying to converse, but Riya was totally distracted. She was wondering what we were up to.

They stopped near a dhaba called Twinkle's Delight. We parked further away from them. We exchanged fives as I assessed the location. Getting off the bike we walked towards the dhaba, which faced the highway and had a spacious lawn in front. I was quite surprised by their choice of eatery for a date. My only guess was that Vidit liked the privacy that came with the location or the long drive in the Beetle. I envisaged that most of Vidit's late-night beer parties would be here. Since it was her first date, Riya must have been subdued.

The dhaba had five charpoys laid at a little distance from each other. There were planks on either side to hold the platters. There were some tables as well. They took a table and we took a charpoy very close to them.

Riya sat with her back to us. She had avoided approaching us as she knew we could turn nasty. You see, every action has an equal and opposite reaction!

Vidit would not have expected this from us. But that's what I wanted! He messed with us. I wanted to flash 'Expect the unexpected' in big bold letters.

We were seated within earshot. Initially it was a casual conversation. Then I heard him boast of the land he owned on Mysore road. He said he owned a chicken farm.

Manish and I had lots to talk. We laughed loudly every now and then. That is how it was when Riya used to be with us as well. Riya seemed to close her ears once when we laughed over a joke banging the planks and Manish rolled off the cot and sat on the floor holding his stomach.

A lean boy with a soiled baniyan came out to take the order. He walked up to our opposition party's table.

Riya ordered rumali rotis and tawa baingan. She ordered a lassi as well. Vidit ordered chicken gravy and some rotis. He looked at Riya meaningfully and said, 'The spicier the food on my plate, the better I like it.'

'Make it extra spicy,' he told the server.

'Make it extra spicy,' I imitated in a goofy voice.

Manish laughed. Vidit gaped at me. I yawned at his face.

We ordered phulkas and rajma. We took one fresh lime soda between the two of us.

We sat close to a tree. The branches swayed now and then. It was a little cloudy and it had rained the previous night. If not for the demon sitting in front, it was a pleasant afternoon.

As I sat and enjoyed the surroundings, Manish seemed to have woven a plot in his mind. He had made up his mind to give Vidit a taste of his own medicine.

He unbuttoned the sleeves of his full-sleeved shirt, folded it, pumped his arms to show off his well-built muscles and gestured to Vidit to come down and fight. Vidit looked agitated. Obviously, Riya could not see us. But she saw the weird look on Vidit's face.

My jaw dropped. 'Why did you do that?' I asked.

'Wait and watch,' Manish said and immediately lay down on the cot, cradled his head in his hands and gazed at the sky. He was super quick. Meanwhile, Vidit was blabbering, 'That sicko! Your friend Manish wants to fight with me.'

'What!' Riya was loud. She turned back. I sat unperturbed gazing into nowhere, leaning back on my shoulders, and Manish looked like he was ready to doze off.

'Don't be so intimidated by them, Vidit. I know they are irritating but Manish looks ready to doze off. Please don't imagine things.' Riya sounded a little irritated with Vidit.

'Get up, you lazybones,' I said pulling Manish up and adding authenticity to the scene. He sat up, even as Riya was looking.

It was working. The minute Riya turned her back to us we gave each other a hi-five, got up and did a quick dance to highlight Vidit's defeat. Vidit sat fuming and pointed towards us again with an expression which read, *You won't believe what I just saw.* Riya turned again. She saw me walking slowly with my hands behind my back, looking at the vehicles passing by. Manish was walking a few steps to get a closer look at a cute white calf with black and brown spots tied a few feet away from all the seats.

'Now what!' said Riya exasperated.

'They were dancing? They were making fun of me,' Vidit whined petulantly.

'Vidit, relax!' Riya said.

'I am going to teach them a lesson. I have seen enough.' Vidit got up from his table and walked briskly towards Manish. He obviously could not hit me. He wanted to mow down Manish. But Manish was strong enough to easily bring Vidit down. I was a little tense in spite of that. It was not a good feeling to see them fight, and the brawl could turn spiteful.

Riya had left her table. She was calling out to Vidit.

Vidit was mad with rage. All he wanted to do was to bash up Manish. He charged, slipped on something unexpected, a squashed mango which lay on the ground. To my pleasure and Riya's disgust he lost his balance and fell face first in some slushy mud. Manish and I burst into laughter. Riya stood there like a frozen statue.

Vidit got up slowly. House flies kissed the mud on his face. He started walking towards the road with his hands stretched. He trod cautiously, trying to find his way. He evidently couldn't see where he was going. If I had the power, I would have wanted to peek into his brain to know what he felt. His face was so covered with mud that we couldn't see his expression. The black jeans he wore with a blue T-shirt now looked like they belonged to a 'before wash' detergent ad on TV.

We saw Vidit grit his teeth and he charged towards Manish to bash him up. But Riya's reflexes were quick this time. She stood in front of Vidit and screamed, 'Stop it! Enough is enough. What is the matter with you? Leave him alone. Stop behaving like a moron.'

Vidit, for sure, did not expect this. He looked ready to slap Riya. He definitely didn't look like a guy who could tolerate women talking to him in a loud voice. But he controlled his anger. This was disturbing to me. I always feel people who spit out anger are better than the ones who bottle it up as they can be dangerous. I did not want him to take it out on Riya in any other way.

He slowly walked towards the wash area to clean himself up. Riya walked up to us. She markedly didn't look at me. She looked at Manish and said, 'I don't know what you were up to. But there is something I want you to do. I want you to apologize to Vidit.'

Over time she had taken him so much for granted that she wanted him to bend backwards for her again.

'Why should I apologize to your mad boyfriend? First, he turns up naked in front of all the girls, that pervert, them makes it all sound like an accident, and now he has mud all over him. What are you up to with this cartoon, Riya? And why do you even think that I will apologize to such a loser?'

Manish turned and looked at me. My face was grim.

Manish was polite and his voice was authoritative when he spoke again, 'Riya, if you think I am a puppet in your hands and you can pull the strings, sorry. I think it is high time you come out of your illusions and take a look around. Not everything works the way you want, all the time. I have tolerated enough of your temper and misbehaviour in the past, in the name of friendship. But not anymore.'

You go boy! I thought. But I stood there without any expression on my face. Manish sounded so serious that Riya didn't have the guts to talk back. But she had to take it out on someone.

She turned to me and let her tongue fly, 'You slut! You know how to hook boys, don't you? So you have finally learnt the art. And you don't seem to be happy enough with one boyfriend. You have Aadi for weekends and Manish for weekdays. Good work, babe. You have exceeded expectations.'

Manish spoke before I could open my mouth, 'You know what, Riya, at least I tolerated you hoping you would like me some day. But Saachi had nothing to gain out of all this. She was only trying to get you out of this mess, as she couldn't stand by and see you ruin your life. You are a loser, Riya, bitching about someone who's a friend for life. You don't deserve us. From today you are on your own.'

'Thanks for nothing,' she spat. 'My well-wishers! It would be a great help if you kept away. Thank God, at least now you understood what I want.'

We were in no mood to make ourselves any more of a spectacle than we needed to—as it was, all eyes were on us— and we left the place. On the way back I told Manish all about Aadi's role in the striptease and how Aadi had spoken to Vidit and found out his real intentions.

Manish was undoubtedly happy to hear what I told him. Now the whole drama made sense to him.

Manish versus Vidit

⤷

Aadi thoroughly enjoyed the dhaba episode narration over the phone. He said he would have loved to be around. He also cautioned me to be careful of Vidit.

Vidit and Manish acted like territorial animals, keeping intruders—each other—out of their personal space. I could visualize them growling, baring their teeth, ready to pounce whenever they crossed ways. Vidi, for sure, was waiting for the next best chance to get Manish.

Weeks and months passed. We were close to the end of our college years. Riya and Vidit were the talk of the town. They were a Page 3 couple now, and were hardly seen on campus unless absolutely necessary. The semester had passed by. Her seventh semester results were the lowest compared to all her previous semesters.

Even when Riya came to college, she made pretty sure to ward off any conversation with anyone. Manish and I didn't exist in her world anymore.

Aadi called me on a Thursday afternoon. He was on Fergusson College Road, a happening place in Pune. He was at Shabari, a restaurant which served an amazing Maharashtrian thaali. He had spoken about this place many times before.

'Hey Saachi, where do you plan to have dinner this Saturday?' Aadi asked.

'Hmm? At home, where else,' I promptly replied. There were no plans of Aadi coming over that weekend.

'How about a five star dinner at Windsor Manor?' he asked.

'Oh yeah! I forgot. The owner of Windsor Manor is my grandfather's second brother's third wife's cousin, four times removed. He's invited me for dinner this weekend, how could I forget!' I said giggling.

'Good. I had planned to take you there for dinner this weekend.'

'Are you coming to Bengaluru this weekend?' I was on cloud nine every time he came. But this was new. We never went to fve star hotels. His principle was that his dad was rich, not him. I should accept the fact that he would manage his month well within the pocket money his dad gave, and never asked for more. We always ate in simple places and Aadi enjoyed all the eat-outs I took him to in and around Malleshwaram. We made sure to pay in turn as per our pact, actually more of my pact.

'Yes!' he said.

'But why are we going to Windsor?' I asked.

'I got my first pay cheque.' Aadi never sounded so happy before.

'Pay cheque? Are you kidding? You have a full semester of studies to finish.' I was confused.

'Saachi, after I worked on Nitin's bike, I started designing cars and bikes on my system, just for the love of it. My friend Sid happened to see it. His family friend owns a showroom with many brands of cars and bikes. He talked me into showing my designs to his friend's father, who was apparently tired of shelling out dollar equivalents to international designers. He said he would have the parts imported and get my modifications done here. He bought all my designs and I got a heavy cheque. He has asked me to give him more designs.' Aadi sounded thrilled.

'Aadi, you rock! I am so proud of you. I think I should take up jewellery designing as an evening job.' Both of us laughed. I was so happy. I liked Aadi's attitude of being independent. I was really proud of him.

'Aadi, I am very happy. Forget the treat. Why don't you gift your dad and aunty something? Your dad will be very proud of you,' I said.

'I already bought a sari for my aunty. But I don't know what my dad likes of late. We haven't spoken much in years,' Aadi replied.

Aadi didn't speak much about his family and I didn't bring it up as well.

'Saachi, I will be there by five on Saturday. I will come to your place by eight.'

I waited eagerly for the weekend. I updated Manish on Aadi's stroke of luck. Manish was very happy for him too.

Manish, meanwhile, had shown good progress in getting over Riya. No, he didn't take up drinking, didn't grow a beard, didn't wear the same shirt for a week, and didn't get into drugs. I would, now and then, rake up the topic of how he was holding up when I got the feeling that he wanted me to. He would then open up on his hidden painful love disaster. He had definitely tied his hopes to this golden deer. But now he realized the deer did not exist. He did not blame anyone. He would tell me how he was taking one day at a time. He said when he looked around he saw many things that still inspired him. Besides, he added, if one could get all fired up over something or someone, one should also have the ability to face reality and cool off, if need be. He was not a loser to get passionate now about destroying himself or Riya.

The wheel kept turning. We were busy preparing for the finals and the campus interviews which would start the next week. I had decided to gain two years of experience in information technology, and then pursue higher studies through my earnings and not burden my dad anymore. My dad was not very happy about it. At the same time he knew I was someone who had a mind of my own and wouldn't budge easily.

It was Friday. We attended a pre-placement session on the companies that could come in for recruitment. Professors Jagdeesh, Sharada, Somesh and our HOD Prof. Menon were present to brief us. There was a lecture on how we should dress on those days, how we should conduct ourselves, the do's and don'ts, how to face the various rounds, and what were the terms and conditions involved when being appointed, etc.

Riya sat without any interest through the session.

Through the lecture I couldn't help but notice Vidit busy scribbling something on a paper. I was surprised that there was even a remote chance of him taking notes. He was pathetic in studies, and with time we had realized he was senior to us by two years. The session ended with the previous year's success stories to motivate the students. Prof. Somesh walked through the class briskly distributing some brochures.

The professors wished us luck and left the class. I walked slowly out of the class, reading through the brochures. Manish walked out, followed by Vidit. For some reason Riya sat there with her head bent and looked restless. Her cheeks seemed to have lost their colour. She looked pale, like she had had a fight with Vidit. But it was no more my business.

Just as I looked up I saw Vidit holding a white sheet and it read in bold letters: *'You stinking Profs! I am hired!!! I am the head of toilet cleaners at Pereira's. I have a fancy uniform too!'*

Oh shit! I thought. *What the hell is he up to?*

The professors who had left the class had gathered in the middle of the hallway and were totally engrossed in their discussion on where they were on the arrangements for the next week. Prof. Somesh and Prof. Jagadeesh were updating Prof. Menon on their plans.

Manish was approaching them. Vidit seemed to pick up pace to reach him. I watched in disgust, not knowing how to react from where I stood.

I quickly pulled out my cell from my bag and tried to call Manish. I was checking on Vidit at the same time as I frantically looked for Manish's number.

Vidit was quick as lightning. He lifted his hand and tried to stick the sheet on Manish's back. I opened my mouth to call out to Manish across the hallway. It would mean getting everyone else's attention, but definitely faster than making a call.

But I didn't have to. It looked like Vidit was being hounded by all the unlucky stars. The brochures in Manish's hand slipped and scattered on the ground. He bent to pick them up and Vidit's white paper with its foul message got stuck to Prof. Menon's back.

These are the moments where you don't know whether to laugh or cry. The Romeo gang members Sandeep, Akshay and Sagar were right behind me and they had noticed the whole drama. We stood there looking at each other's faces.

Manish, oblivious to what happened, walked past the group of professors. Vidit quickly took the first stairs down as he realized the outcome could be unpleasant if he got caught.

∾

The twist in the tale that day was when the classes for third year that were being conducted in the adjacent rooms dispersed for a break. Students started pouring out of these rooms. The abusive hoarding stuck to the HOD's back made all of them giggle.

As expected, all the giggles and murmurs caught Prof. Menon's attention and he turned and roared, 'What is so funny?'

Prof. Menon's back now faced the other professors. Prof. Somesh moved close to Prof. Menon's back and read every word, very distinctly, aloud. Prof. Menon's eyes were wide open and looked like fireballs as Prof. Somesh read aloud, 'You stinking Profs! I am hired!!! I am the head of toilet cleaners at Pereira's. I have a fancy uniform too!'

Prof. Menon stood there frozen at the spot. The students fell silent and watched with fear.

'Who was it?' he roared. It seemed to echo across the campus.

Well, it was time for our Romeo gang heroes to avenge their hatred on Vidit who had looted their lady love. They walked up to the professors and narrated what they had witnessed in detail.

Prof. Menon realized Manish was the intended target and not him. Manish's blackboard proposal in a full class was a famous story. Riya being irregular with her attendance in class and being seen with the infamous Vidit was a bigger story.

Prof. Menon sent Sandeep to find Vidit and Manish and summon them to his chamber.

Riya who had walked out of the class saw what had unfolded and looked terribly upset. Her face was ashen white. The whole crowd made her aware of every step she took till the exit. Within minutes I could see her Beetle zip off the campus, raising the dust, as I stood in the corridor looking out and waiting for Manish to come out of Prof. Menon's chamber.

Manish and Vidit walked out of the chamber in a few minutes, and Vidit looked as ferocious as a dog whose tail had been freshly cut. He warned Manish before he left, 'I will get you next time.'

Manish replied, 'I am sooo scared,' sarcastically.

Manish said HOD Menon had fined Vidit ₹5,000 for lack of attendance, and declared him ineligible to participate in campus recruitment.

Manish, on the other hand, was informed in a much lower tone that his records were great and that the HOD had many hopes for him. He asked him to stay away from all these trivial issues and concentrate more on his goals.

I let out a deep sigh and put my face down.

He asked, 'What happened?'

I told Manish that I had seen Riya upset in the class, and how she had stormed out of the campus, and that things were not right between her and Vidit.

Manish convinced me that we should not even begin to walk down that path.

'Like she says, she is old enough to handle it. Let it pass. For all you know, you will see them walk hand in hand tomorrow. So let's not make it any of our business.'

I was glad Aadi was coming down. It would take my mind off all this. I spent the Saturday morning preparing for the interviews. I surfed the net to get more info on common interview questions, interview tips, etc.

The aroma of mom's freshly made Mysore masala dosa filled the house. It is amazing when you come out of your bathroom after a good shower on a holiday and smell good food. You are in no hurry to gulp the food down and you can eat it either reading a newspaper or listening to music. I realized how hungry I was.

I had noticed my mom glowing of late. She was thoroughly enjoying the yoga classes and there was a lot of change in her energy levels. I was very happy to see her take out time to keep herself fit. I used to catch my dad lingering around the kitchen these days singing Kishore Kumar's love songs, trying to get her attention.

Mom would blush but knew how to punish him as well. Whenever he came to the kitchen she would make him peel carrots, sort out the greens, peel cucumbers, etc.

I would laugh at their 'Old is Gold' kind of romance and embarrass them either by coughing and indicating that I was right across the hall, or by increasing the TV volume or singing loudly. I kind of felt shy catching them romance. But all this also made me believe in relationships.

That evening Aadi came home at 7:00 p.m. instead of 8:00 p.m., as per the plan. He had not bothered to call earlier.

I had got back from the parlour fifteen minutes earlier. I wanted to look presentable at dinner as well as at the interview. I was painting my nails, sitting in my shorts on a sofa, with my legs propped up on the side table.

My mom answered the door and let Aadi in. I didn't turn back as I expected it to be my dad.

'Aadi,' my mom exclaimed, indicating her happiness to see him. She was very happy to know that Aadi was showing interest in designing bikes and was doing so along with his studies.

They both hugged. I was shocked to hear his name. I was not expecting him for another hour, at the least. I had never shown so much of my skin earlier to him.

Aadi glanced at me and my bare legs as he hugged my mom. He had some carry-bags in his hand. My mom kissed his forehead and said she was proud of him.

I grabbed the sofa cover and tied it around my waist. Mom laughed loudly. Aadi put down the bags, hugged my mom from behind, and whistled as I ran from there to get into something less revealing. I could hear Aadi say 'Ouch!' as my mom pulled his ear for his prank. I pulled on my track pants and almost ran into Aadi, who whispered, 'I never knew you had such sexy legs.' That was it. It was time for a kung fu hustle. Aadi escaped and ran to the terrace. I had to use my wit rather than energy.

I called out, 'Dad', as if he was present there.

Aadi, startled, stepped further into the terrace and saw nobody; turning, he grabbed my hand. I started hitting him hard. He caught both my hands and pushed me against a wall.

I struggled to free my hands and hit him again. He was too strong.

All off a sudden I realized Aadi had softened down and was looking into my face with a small smile on his face.

I stopped struggling. I was now conscious of every part of my body.

Aadi was leaning over me. His tall frame towered over me. I was pressed against his chest. My legs were between his legs, supporting my body that was leaning against the wall. I could smell my nail paint and his cologne. Neither of us spoke. I had goose bumps. My vocal chords seemed incapable of producing any sound at all.

He slowly released his hold and his hand slid down every inch of my arms till my elbows. It was electrifying. It was not that Aadi had never held me before. We held hands all the time. But those were times when we felt like fast friends. This time it was different. I didn't know how and why though.

He leaned further towards my face as if to kiss me. I could hear my heart beat loud and clear. I didn't know what he had in mind. This was not Aadi. No matter how much I wanted it, I didn't want him to get into anything that he was not ready for, and then feel bound to me because of it.

I forced my vocal chords to function and squeaked, 'Aadi.'

His expression didn't change.

I gave it another shot. 'Aadi', this time a little firmer.

'Aadi, you are scaring me,' I managed a whole sentence.

To my shock Aadi burst out laughing, came forward and gave me a boyish hug and said, 'See, that is why I tell you, you can never be a girl. If you were a girl you would not have stopped me today from kissing you. Girls die for one kiss from me.' He ruffled my hair as he spoke.

This was a total twist in the tale. A hard core romantic movie had suddenly turned into an uncalled-for comedy, making me feel like a fool.

I had tears in my eyes but the darkness hid them. Aadi never took me seriously. Even though I enjoyed it that way, there were times when I would grow weary of it.

I didn't know where I was heading, and I knew for a fact that he was always heading in the opposite direction. Aadi had girls flocking around him all the time and boys envied him equally. There were girls throwing themselves at him at parties, but Aadi restrained himself. He gently but firmly would make it clear to them that he was not interested.

'I will never kiss anyone who is not in love with me, Aadi,' I said, as I freed myself and walked towards the stairs.

'Come again?' Aadi pulled my shoulders and made me face him.

I changed my sentence. 'Why did you even think that I would let any old guy kiss me?'

'So I am any old guy?' his eyes narrowed.

I could never read Aadi's mind. There were times when I felt he was in love with me and he acted like I was his possession, but many a time when I felt I was just his friend, a good friend and nothing else.

'Maybe not any old guy, but why would I let you kiss me, Aadi?' I spoke in a stern voice.

'Come on, Saachi. It was just one of my practical jokes. Why are you taking it so seriously?' Aadi gave me an uncomfortable smile.

'Are we going for dinner?' I changed the topic. I started walking down the stairs and reached the living-room.

'Oh yes! I came early as I wanted you to wear this.'

He pulled out a chiffon salwar-kameez that was sky blue in colour. It had embroidery on the neckline in dark blue silk thread which complmented the body of the salwar. It was beautiful.

'Why did you bother!' He knew I was uncomfortable with gifts.

He replied with a smile.

My mom loved the dress. My dad walked into the house, 'How are you, handsome?' That is how he addressed him always.

'Not as handsome as you, Uncle,' was Aadi's usual reply. They shook hands.

'Congrats, my boy! So you are as good at dressing up girls as dressing up bikes. You have taste,' my dad winked, looking at the dress Aadi was holding in his hands.

'PJ, Dad,' I said, rolling my eyes.

'Does it mean please joke?' asked my dad.

'No! Poor joke, Dada,' I replied.

༄

Aadi had got a mehendi coloured Maharashtrian silk sari for my mom from Lakshmi Road, the best street for shopping in Pune, and a pullover for my dad from Camp, another area with good shopping and called Camp because it houses much of the Cantonment area.

'Aadi, I think you went overboard. Looks like you spent all that you made,' I said.

'No, I told you it was a fat cheque. My friend's father said these days there was a lot of demand for modifications and it was getting tough to cater to teenage needs. Now he has a website with my designs on it, and he can give the customers a choice.' Aadi was excited.

'What did you buy for yourself and your dad?' I asked.

'I bought a new mobile.' He showed me. It was cool. 'And I got my dad a watch,' he smiled.

I was happy to hear that.

I quickly dressed up and we left for dinner. Aadi complimented me, saying that I looked gorgeous.

We walked through the big hall at the entrance and the whitewalled, glass-ceiling dining-rooms of Windsor Manor. Aadi had booked a poolside table and candles shone from a designer silver candle-stand. There were beautiful orchids in a small vase. The table looked perfect.

The steward pulled the chair out for me. Aadi sat across the table. Aadi looked handsome in a white shirt and blue jeans. His eyes looked darker in the candlelight and his thick lashes made them look irresistible.

Aadi smiled. I realized that my eyes were fixed on his face and I was not talking.

'I know I look handsome,' he said.

'Ah! Pompous,' I replied. 'I was just thinking which eye

shadow and lipstick you use,' I said with a mischievous smile. Aadi is really fair and has red lips.

'I guess the lipstick got there when we kissed,' he smiled.

'We didn't. Aadi! Stop it. What is with you and kissing today?' I looked angry.

'Nothing. I was just answering your question,' he said.

Aadi ordered mocktails and a veg platter.

I placed a small gift-wrapped box on the table. 'This is for you,' I said.

'What is this?' Aadi asked.

'It is our custom to gift a Ganeshji idol to family and friends who start work for the first time,' I said.

'Wow! That's very thoughtful of you, Saachi.' He was touched.

He opened the gift. I had selected a Ganesh pendant for him.

'This is gold!' he exclaimed.

'It is jewellery,' I smiled.

'Okay, you can sleep with me one night,' Aadi chuckled, reminding me of the debate we had on bikes and jewellery.

'Looks like you're going to eat your dinner in the pool,' I glared at him.

We spoke more nonsense and then some more nonsense. Aadi then said he had treated Mahi and gang, which included his friend Sid who had introduced him to the dealer before he came here. He had taken them to Chandni Chowk which was a hillock with many restaurants on the outskirts of Pune. Aadi spoke a lot about Mahi these days. By now, I was close enough to Aadi to ask him some personal questions.

'Aadi, do you like Mahi?' I asked.

'Of course, that is why she is my friend,' he said.

'I mean like, *like*, Aadi. Do you have feelings for her?' I asked.

'Hey! Can you spell this out?' he asked.

Aadi sang a tongue-twister from his schooldays.

'I feel a feel,

A funny feel I feel,

If you feel the feel I feel,

I feel the feel you feel.'

'Aadi, stop being a ten-year-old. Can you ever be serious?'

'Why should I?' he asked.

I sat silently. He realized I was annoyed. He never answered any of my questions directly.

Aadi sat looking thoughtful for a while. He then touched my hand across the table.

'I will tell you one of the reasons why I am so indifferent towards these things,' he said. 'My best friend Sanju from school was a male version of Riya. He lost his heart to a girl in Class 12. They were seeing each other. They were the worst pair ever. They fought over everything as time passed but would patch up again.' Aadi looked into the distance, his gaze unfocused.

'When we were in third-year engineering they got married, as their parents realized that they were going around and wanted to get the girl married. It was the biggest mistake. I told him many times that they were not compatible. But he would not listen. He said these things were common in relationships and they both loved each other a lot.' Aadi stared at the pool and shifted uncomfortably in his seat.

'Beyond a point I could not interfere. I mean, it was too personal. They quit their studies and took up odd jobs to run the house. They did not have enough maturity to deal with real life issues. Things went from bad to worse. The boy's family interfered every now and then. They would visit their house on some pretext and insult the girl. My friend was also very short-tempered, and their relationship began to get seriously affected.' Aadi let out a deep sigh.

'Now they are divorced. He has come back home but has started drinking. His dad has enough to support him. His ex-wife was not accepted by her parents. She lives on her own. She is finding it hard to survive. Now she works for my dad as he was kind enough to understand, and she is doing a good job. I am also urging her to finish her studies. But all said and done, she goes back to an empty house with neither her family nor her husband to support her. Her life lies before her as a big question mark.' Aadi paused.

'You date girls behind your parents'? back as it is considered a sin to be seen with the other gender. Then you are afraid of facing the world if you break up. Isn't the phrase "break-up" much better than the word "divorce" or even "suicide"? Why can't we handle these things with some dignity? If a boy and a girl decide to fall in love, they also have the right to decide to get out of it. Why are there so many suicides? Why don't parents educate their kids about it? Why don't they talk openly? Why was his wife never accepted back? How many men will be ready to give her a life? There is just one life, Saachi. I hate it when people act foolish and screw lives up.'

The more I heard of it, the more of his aversion to the topic I sensed. It was like he was mistakenly born in a society like ours. I did agree that we need to show the same strength and power to handle a broken relationship that we show while diving headlong into it, but hey, these things happen! That does not mean you blame each other or spoil each other's life.

Who likes to see headlines like 'Boy commits suicide after tiff with girlfriend', 'Teenage boy stabs girlfriend on suspicion of infidelity', 'Girl in love kills herself due to forced marriage'?

There are much better causes to lose your precious life than these. There are youngsters enrolling in the army, navy and air force and losing their lives. They are our heroes.

Every student should be counselled in college through various seminars where famous psychologists, psychiatrists and counsellors are invited to teach youngsters to face life head on. Just seminars about technology do not help.

At the end of the day all students at this vulnerable age are prone to romantic feelings, the fear of being left behind compared to their friends, failing exams, failing interviews, having to turn their back on what they are passionate about in order to earn fat salaries, and not being able to afford studies abroad. Even college days, considered to be golden days, have their own problems and issues.

I would say parents, too need to be counselled on how to be friends with their kids, how to talk their language, where and how to draw a line. This would go a long way in shaping their kids' future.

College professors and lecturers cannot treat students as they did in the good old times, where they could even hit students in college or insult them in an open class. Times have changed. Instead of fretting and frowning over the new generation, they should employ their experience and help to mould the students in a tactful way, instead of talking of examples from the past.

'What is the other reason, Aadi?' I asked coming back to the world. By now, I was clear on his take on what he thought of love, marriage and relations. But at the same time, I was sure there must be a stronger reason.

If he didn't want to get married just when he started seeing a girl, he could very well make it clear to her while dating, and take it the way he desired. It was not such an irresolvable issue. There was definitely something which was, for sure, beyond his control.

There was a long silence.

'It is my dad,' Aadi swallowed as he spoke.

'Your dad?' I was shocked.

'Yes, my dad,' he said.

'What about him?' I was confused.

'Sorry, Saachi! I am not comfortable talking about it now,' Aadi said.

'Okay, let's stick to bikes and jewellery. It is much easier to talk about them,' I smiled. We had spent an evening, which could have turned romantic, talking social issues. Now what did I expect?

That night as I lay in bed I replayed my close brush with the romantic tryst I had come so close to having with Aadi. I, for a second, put behind the sad story he shared with me and the reasons why he was against relationships. I dreamt what would have happened that evening if Aadi did love me.

Aadi leaned over to kiss me. My lips trembled. My cheeks were cold. I looked deep into his eyes. His lips craved to feel mine. His hands cupped my face. I turned my face and leaned on the wall, unable to look him in the eye. His fingers turned my face. He made me look at him.

He rubbed my cheek as if to familiarize me with his touch. He kissed my right cheek. I took his left hand and kissed his palm. He moved forward to kiss my lips. I could feel a love flame engulf us. I could feel my stomach somersaulting.

I was too shy to let him kiss my lips. I moved quickly and leaned on the wall with my back to him and my palms on the wall on either side. He smiled. He moved my hair over my left shoulder. He moved the tip of his index finger on the right side of my neck. I was pushing all my weight on the wall with my hands. He clasped my hands with his hands, bent over and slowly planted kisses on my neck.

I never knew my neck was so sensitive. He was waking every unknown sensual feeling in me.

I couldn't take it anymore. I turned towards him and hugged him tight, my face hiding in his chest. He held me tight as if to comfort me. I knew I was giving him a tough time. But he was very patient and warm. His gentleness soothed me. He slowly pulled me away from his chest. I was looking down. He lifted my chin with one finger. I was looking at his face. My cheeks were hot now.

He took my right hand and made me move it over his lips. They were perfect. They were mine. This handsome gentle romantic creature was mine. I slowly moved my fingers on his face. His clean-shaven face was smooth. He now clasped my face with sweet dominance..

I could no more resist. Before I realized it, he was kissing my lips gently. I kissed him back. My hand was in his hair which felt soft, and escaped between my fingers. The kiss picked up pace and now we were both in another world. I could feel his lips, his tongue. It grew stronger and stronger till I felt giddy.

My cell beeped indicating a message. It was Aadi. It read: 'Gud nite chipmunk.'

I covered my face in my blanket and hid behind it as if I had sinned. I let out a sigh and struggled to fall asleep.

Riya Grows Up!

Sunday afternoon, Aadi was all set to fly back to Pune. He wanted to meet me briefly before he left. We met at Coffee Day. Aadi gave me gyan as I sat relishing every sip of my cold coffee, 'Devil's Own', with whipped cream to top it.

'Don't let them realize you are dumb. For one day just pretend to be smart.'

'I will try. But don't you think your influence on me is quite visible?' I asked.

'For Pete's sake, don't argue with them the way you argue with me,' he said.

'Naah…I won't. I will take my recruiter on a date and sweet-talk him,' I pretended to blush.

'Hmm, then arguing sounds better in my head.'

That evening my dad left for a walk in a garden two blocks from my place. There were still a few silent lanes spared in Malleshwaram, in spite of the sudden influx of people. Areas like Malleshwaram, Jayanagar, Gandhi Bazaar—some of the oldest localities in Bengaluru—housed some of the city's oldest bungalows which would never lose their charm.

These buildings captured the essence of Old Bengaluru for us. Most of these houses are painted cream with tiled roofs. The ventilators are usually circular and the windows are four-paned and have colourful glasses on top. The bungalows have a small lawn with mango trees in them. The metal gates creak when opened, due to age. I never fail to feel a tingle in my stomach when I spot these bungalows.

My mom kept her promise and demonstrated the various asanas she had learnt in her yoga class. First, she started with some warm up postures, followed by Surya Namaskara.

I sat gaping at how flexible my mom was when she balanced herself in trikonasana. She further made me gasp in awe as she performed parivritta trikonasana with great ease and elegance. It was a treat to my eyes. At the same time I felt ashamed about being glued to the computer and not doing anything about my fitness.

I couldn't hold back my admiration and clapped like a small kid who sees her mom win the Mrs World competition on TV. The doorbell rang indicating a visitor.

I opened the door. I could not believe my eyes. Riya stood there with swollen red eyes and a noticeable bruise just beneath her left eye.

'Saachi, who is at the door?' my mom called out.

'Riya,' I said. Even I could hardly hear my voice, leave alone my mom. I was numb. My mom came to check on me. She was as surprised as me to see Riya standing at the door.

'Riya, what happened? Are you alright, child? Come in.' Riya stood there with tears welling up in her eyes, waiting for me to call her in.

Reasoning failed as I saw her in that state. My anger seemed extinct. My self-respect went on a walk and empathy dominated.

My motor cells responded and helped me to hold her hand and lead her into the seating area in our living-room. My mom turned the fan speed up by a notch. I guess she knew the room was bound to get heated up. She noiselessly placed a water jar and two glasses on the table.

She excused herself on the pretext of joining my father on his walk. She whispered into my ears as I followed her to close the door, 'There is baked corn in the oven. Heat it up and give it to her. She likes corn. You will find chaat masala in the refrigerator.'

I adored my mom for these little things that she did for me and my friends.

'Mom, I love you,' I whispered back, and gave a quick peck on her cheek.

'I know,' my mom winked. I could hear Riya sniff as I entered the living area.

I sat beside her on a couch. There were thousands of questions popping up in my head. *Why was she here? More importantly, why was she bruised? What will she say? What should I say?*

Both of us had not uttered a word in the last ten minutes. Riya sat there crying, wiping her eyes now and then, and twisting her fingers the rest of the time. Her nose was red by now. Her face closely resembled a tomato.

I tried hard to look all wise and strong. I was just a month older than her. But I always felt like I was responsible for her and older to her by at least a few years. No matter how much I tried, tears rolled down my cheeks too. I didn't know why I was crying. Seeing her cry so uncontrollably brought tears to my eyes.

She saw me cry and cried more incessantly now. I gave her some tissues.

It took a while for her to calm down. I let her cry as I knew it would make her feel better. 'Saachi, I am sorry,' she said, her voice still very shaky.

'You better be,' I laughed, wiping my tears.

'I was such an idiot,' she said.

'I know!' I tapped her fingers.

'You are still your same old irritating self,' she smiled.

'I'm not going to change,' I assured her with a naughty smile. I just wanted to ease the situation.

'So, do you want to tell me what happened?' I finally asked when I felt she was ready for it.

'It…it was all wrong. So wrong,' she choked.

I poured some water and gave her the glass. She slowly sipped on it.

'I thought it was love. I fell crazily for Vidit. There was no stopping it. Of course, there were one or two mishaps at the party and dhaba.' She let out a small laugh. 'After our big fight at the dhaba, I was happy that I got rid of you and Manish.' There was no point in questioning why she behaved the way she did with us. We knew her insecurities and that in her heart she also knew that keeping us meant losing Vidit.

She continued, 'It was like a dream. We spent more and more time with each other. Everything looked rosy in the beginning. We went for long drives, late nights, movies; I got him lot; of gifts, I got one or two from him as well; shopping, discos and so on and so forth.' She paused, as the good times she thought had she spent with Vidit must have played in front of her eyes.

'Is this one of his gifts too?' I pointed at her bruise, bringing her to the present.

'Yes!' she sobbed again. My worst fear had come true. He

had actually hit her. I really wished that I knew magic and I could vaporize him into thin air, and this was not a joke.

She continued with a heavy breath. 'The fairy tale didn't last for long. I realized he was more of Jekyll and Hyde rather than any Prince Charming. He compelled me to get my Beetle for all the drives. He even took it away for partying with his friends. I used to find used tissues with lipstick marks on them when he returned the car. He said they were his friends' girlfriends'.'

She did her best to control her sobbing.

'I never once saw him offering to pay for our lunches or dinners. He would drive us down to posh hotels and resorts saying he wanted to try the pub there, or the sea food was good, and stuff like that, and would simply pass the bill on to me. He took me out just once, for our first date in the dhaba where Manish and you had followed us. I ended up with an upset tummy.'

I passed her some more tissues.

'This lavish behaviour was fine with me up to a point. But there came a time when I started sensing that he was attracted to the wealth that surrounded me, more than me. I was only helping him get popular. But I still had hopes, mostly in me than him. I felt my love could change him. I finally sat down with him and told him my future plans.' There was a lot of disappointment in her face now.

'I told him how I felt about my parents, how I have secretly wished, for many years now, to disown them, how I wanted to make a life with him without their support, how I never wanted to be an engineer.'

'Okay…?' I paused.

'Everything changed from that day. He would pick on me for everything, the way I dressed, the way I spoke, my relationship with Manish before, any guy I even accidently looked at or any guy who looked at me.' She seemed to recollect those bad times again.

'He would smoke a lot and when I asked him not to, he would say that if I wanted to be with him, I should not order him what to do. He would force me to drink and buy him drinks. At one instance I put my foot down and refused to pay.' She looked at my face.

'Guess what he did?' she asked.

'What?' I was so angry. I knew whatever he would have done would be sick.

'He left me at the table, walked out and didn't turn back. He did not bother to apologize as well. I had no say in anything. He started using bad language and spoke ill of my parents. He called my mom a whore and my dad impotent. It was hell, Saachi.' She wept into her hands.

I knew Vidit was a control freak. But he definitely shocked me.

'But what was the reason for him to behave like that?' It was not sinking in for me.

'The same reason I told you. I started rebelling against his ways, and whenever he said we would break up, I would insist that I wanted it to work. I used to find faults in myself and apologize to him even though I hadn't done anything wrong. I just couldn't stand the word 'break up' and felt that I would do anything under the sun to make this work. I guess he had thought I was easy to get off with. But it didn't turn out that way. I was quite adamant.' She was gesturing a lot with her hands now.

'You are such an idiot. What was the necessity for you to take all that shit? Why didn't you let go?' I expressed my irritation at her stupidity.

'It was me against me, Saachi. I didn't want to be my mom. I always blamed her for not trying enough about making her relationships work. I didn't want to be like her. I thought I was different. I didn't want to give up on love.' She looked so innocent.

'He never loved you, Riya,' I said softly, in a concerned tone.

'What do you mean? Why do you say that? He did...'

I stopped her midway and narrated the whole party saga and how Aadi had managed to pull out the truth from his mouth.

'That sick bastard! Why didn't you tell me, Saachi?' she asked. She got up and started walking up and down the hall. She was very angry.

'What did you think I was trying to do when I came to talk to you every time? You were in no mood to listen.' I showed my disappointment. My head was doing its best to follow her and match up to her speed, as she moved to and fro in front of me.

I had to tell her now. Even now she was thinking all this might just be due to some misunderstandings between them, and did not know Vidit's true intentions.

'Now everything is falling into place.' She thought for a while.

'Why did he hit you?' I asked.

'No, he didn't hit me,' she said. She stopped and looked at me.

'He didn't hurt you? I thought you said it was his gift.' I was confused.

'If he had beaten me up I would have taken him to the police,' she said. 'We had a fight over what happened at college. I was angry with him for trying to frame Manish. I was pissed with him for how he used my name and how it didn't matter to him. He said I anyway never wanted to be a Pereira, so what is the worry all about, and walked out banging the door on my face, and I got hit by the swinging door,' she concluded.

I was glad that he had not hit her. But I was sure that he was capable of it.

'So why did you decide to meet me?' I asked. Riya held my hand at this point. She gently rubbed it. Her action spoke a thousand words of apology.

'Saachi, I was very confused. I didn't know what I was doing was right or wrong. You are the only one who tolerates all my nonsense. I know fights are common in a relationship. My parents fight too but I didn't know how to handle all this. I am glad I came here. Now I know his intentions.' She was still very angry.

'Calm down, Riya. All is well that ends well.'

'No, Saachi. It has not ended. I need to end it.' She sat down on the couch holding her forehead.

'In all this, Saachi, you know what else I realized?' She looked at me.

'What?' I asked slowly.

'Mistakes happen. I always blamed my parents for not being able to tolerate each other. Saachi, it is really difficult to tolerate someone you are not in love with or think you are in love with, but actually are not.' Her words were more of introspection.

'There was nothing common between them, and no matter how much they tried, they could not please each other. How long can you fool each other?' She looked at my face to see if I was with her. I nodded knowingly.

'Sometimes, I feel, my mom behaves the way she does because she has to cover up. She needs to show that she is happy in her materialistic world. A world in which she believes there is no place for emotions, as they can only hurt.' Riya lent back on the sofa and stretched her legs, relaxing.

'My dad had no time for her. He thought she was happy because he provided her with all creature comforts. Thinking from his point of view there were a whole lot of responsibilities on his head. He was also expanding the business which made him neglect his wife. With time my mom changed. She became very superficial about everything. It was like all her feelings died down. To date she is like that.'

Riya, all of a sudden, seemed very mature. I was happy she was seeing the positive side of the mishap in her life. She was able to understand her parents much better now.

'I remember the day my mom left us. She asked my dad to send me with her. But my dad was adamant that I belonged here. Moreover, my mom was not very sure if she could raise me all by herself.' I imagined what it must have been for Riya to witness all that at the age of eleven.

However, I wanted to pull her up.

'You know what, Riya? You have grown up. You don't grow up just because you fall in love.' I smiled, reminding her of what she had said when she mentioned Vidit to me, the very first time.

'I don't think I will ever be in love again,' she grimaced. 'I don't trust love any more.'

Again, her spontaneous conclusions irritated me. I scowled. 'Don't flip between extremes, Riya. You will fall in love again. Just remember, don't be in a hurry to fall in love. Don't confuse your feelings. It is natural to have a crush. It is our age, it is our hormones. It is our mistake to confuse it with love.'

I had her attention now.

'You know what, Riya, let's accept the fact that 90 per cent of boys and girls entering college in India get into something of this kind or the other. Whom are we kidding? It's high time we accepted it. No use living in denial or being all hypocritical about it. These things happen.' I paused.

I gathered momentum, 'But how many of us know how to deal with the ups and downs of it? I think we should never say we love a person until we know him or her quite well. "Love" is the smallest big word, I think. Confusing it with infatuation and screwing your life with your own hands sucks. There is just one life. Please make sure there is a lot more purpose to it than drawing an ultimatum.'

I was only narrating what Aadi had told me in one of our conversations, just a crisper version of it.

'Hmm. Correct. No matter how much progress is seen, the outlook has not changed. Sometimes, it makes it impossible for us to think differently.' She looked like something had just struck her.

'Take my cousin Rinky, for example, who lives in Ireland. Every time I to talk to her she is with a new boyfriend. There, it is normal. It has a downside to it, like not being committed and all that. But why should we imbibe the downside? She doesn't feel shattered and think her life has come to an end just because a relationship didn't work.' She was smiling now, indicating her shift in mood.

'When I tell her I am sorry it didn't work, she says, "Don't be sorry. I learnt scuba diving from him. I learnt piano because of my previous boyfriend." It amazes me how she can look at the positive side of everything. She is getting where she wants to professionally, as well. She doesn't feel harassed over her break-ups.' I was surprised at her perception, especially because Rinky was not her favourite, as her mom always compared her to Rinky.

'God! I can't believe I am admiring her.'

I laughed. 'Don't worry! She doesn't have to know. No one will tell her.'

'So what are you going to do now?' I asked. 'Will you sit and cry for the next one month?'

'No!' she said.

'Will you give up eating and sleeping?' I asked.

'No,' she said. 'I will give up dosas though. I feel they are a high-calorie food,' and she smiled.

'Will you cut your skin to write his name?' I asked.

'No way!' she said, sounding aghast.

'Will you try to commit suicide?' I smiled.

'No. What's with the crazy questions, Saachi—Why should *I* commit suicide? I think I want to teach him a lesson. He has had three girlfriends so far and it is okay, as per him. He tells me to be broad-minded about it, but I am not allowed to even look at other boys. He is such a loser.'

At last! Finally!! I was so happy Riya had seen through this abusive creep. I was happy Riya was here. I was happy she was talking this way. I was happy she knew I was there for her in her bad times. I was happy that her ego didn't come in her way to say sorry and make up, to talk her problems out and not mess up her life any more. It was one happy evening.

'I want to talk to Manish,' she said.

We called him on our speaker phone. First I spoke and then Riya did. He was taken aback to hear her voice. But he was very happy at the end of it. He said he was there if she needed any help.

'What should I do now?' Riya asked.

'For now, avoid meeting him and limit it to phone calls. We will see what we can do.' I said.

'Yeah, you are right. I will just keep it low for a while till we get the right chance. Also, there are two more things I want to do,' she said.

'What?' I asked.

'I am going to call my mom to visit me. This time I will be more patient with her and not complain or ignore her like I always do. Maybe she wants to confide in me as well. I know she loves me. No matter how irritating she is, she always comes down when I ask her to. She shuts down her boutique to be here with me. I will ask her to stay back till I finish my exams.'

'She has a boutique?' I was surprised. Riya had never spoken about it.

'Yes, in London, and do you know what my dream profession is? I want to be a fashion designer. My dad knew it all along, but every time I brought it up, he would say, "Don't act like your mom. Has she been filling all this into your head? Fashion designing is not a profession. You can design your dresses as a hobby. Imagine how good it feels to be called an Electronics Engineer. There are no engineers in our entire family." And so, I was electrocuted, ha ha!!'

We were down on the floor rolling with laughter. I imitated her and she competed. We were back to normal. Riya was back. The fun was back.

We lay down on our backs on the floor, our legs on the sofa and looked at the ceiling, content.

'I think if everything goes well with me and my mom, I will join her in London and help her with her boutique and learn some tricks of the trade as well. She is getting old and I have stayed with my father for too long now. She needs me too, and I am sure she could use some new ideas from a youngster like me. For now, she designs only saris and bridal wear. Maybe I can reinvent her store. Now, since I kept my promise to dad, I am free.' There was new hope in her voice.

'Brilliant, Riya! There is nothing better than pursuing your dreams!' I was so happy she was looking ahead, and so happily too.

'What about you? Have your dreams changed?' she asked.

'No. Two years in IT and then Masters,' I smiled.

'What about Manish?' she asked.

'He doesn't want to work as yet. He is going to go through

the interviews for the experience. But he wants to do his MS abroad,' I said.

'All the best for your interview tomorrow,' she said. 'I don't think it makes sense for me to be there, and also, I don't want to be seen out with this eye.'

A relieved Riya left our house. My mom was very happy; she said she was proud of me because I was mature enough to understand other people's problems and be there when they needed me. If your mom says you are good, you ought to be good, because no one knows you better than her.

That night I filled Aadi in on the pleasant turn of events. He said he was glad Riya was back in her senses.

∽

I was up early the next day. Getting a job was very important to me. I did a quick revision of all the material I had collected. I dressed up in a corporate blue shirt and black trousers. I wore a dark grey stole to go with it. My mom was busy doing a special pooja for me but had laid out breakfast—my favourite rava idlis. I ate quickly, checked myself in the mirror and bid goodbye to my mom and dad. Aadi had given me a wake-up call and wished me luck. He was tenser than I was.

Manish was there when I reached the campus. He said he was having second thoughts about further studies—all the big names in IT were at our campus and it suddenly looked wiser to pick up a great job. But I convinced him to study further when he could afford it. Besides, I reminded him, once you start earning you never know if you will be keen enough to study again or even find the time for that kind of discipline. Money is one of the biggest addictions in life, and though Manish's parents were well-to-do, nevertheless he agreed.

There were five big companies who had come in and we were allowed to choose two out of them for interviews on day one. I chose a firm with branches in five different cities. It was reputed for providing a good working environment.

The interviewer was in his early forties, wore glasses and was clean-shaven. He was going through my papers.

'That's a good track record,' he smiled.

'Thank you, Sir,' I said.

'Please call me Akash,' he smiled again.

'Sure, Sir,' I replied spontaneously. Both of us laughed.

'You have good scores all through. Why do you want to work? Why not study further? You have every chance to get into a good Masters program,' he said

I was diplomatic. 'I want to gain some practical knowledge before I study further.'

'Hmm...'

'You are an Electronics Engineer, so why are you looking for a software job?'

'Well, I want to do Masters in IT. So working in an IT firm will help me,' I said.

Then he fired a whole list of technical questions at me. What were objects, classes, and methods? What was an inheritance? Which operating system had I used and which one was I comfortable with? What were libraries? Could I write SQL queries? How would I rate myself in programming? He asked me to define the software development lifecycle, what are front- and back-end applications —so on and so forth. He gave some examples and asked me to write queries to retrieve those records from the database.

He then asked me to describe my final year project. I had come up with a Knowledge-bank Portal which had student details; options for after-college classes on any topic one was good at; a question-paper database where new questions could be uploaded by anyone looking for an answer, and where people could post Viva questions they faced; reference materials; specializations; a glossary; I and others could post latest gadget details; special offers that were running; and a section dedicated to the professors, the unsung heroes who shape our future.

He asked me if this portal was in use and I helped him to log into the college intranet and access the portal to view the beta version.

At the end he asked me the usual non-IT questions: 'What extra-curricular activities have you contributed to so far?'

I spoke about the 'Know your Junior' program we had brought into operation. The idea was that the top twenty rank-holders from every stream would be tagged to five or ten students from their junior year. They would mentor and guide them and my portal would take care of the mapping issues.

We had started seeing some 'Know your Junior Personally' programs pop up as well, where the boys collected all available information on the junior girls coming into college! It was a better hit than the first one, I can say.

I then spoke about the 'Back to College and Step into Career' program where graduates from our college, now working in various fields, were invited to meet with students and share their experiences.

I told him I was a volunteer for the college festival that was around the corner, and I would be in charge of the medals and certificates, and the bidding stalls.

'What are your hobbies?' he asked.

Hobbies? What are they? Who has the time? Haven't you been listening to me so far, Akash? I thought.

I am doing decently in studies, taking part in various forums, busy making plans to save Riya, meeting Aadi over weekends, watching TV and getting some sleep. But obviously, I couldn't state all this.

So I gave him the most common reply. 'Reading,' I said.

'Which is the last book you read?'

'*Two States*,' I replied promptly.

'Hmm. Chetan Bhagat. He is a hit among college students, isn't he?'

'He is real,' I smiled.

'Why haven't you read any book after that?' he asked.

Who would read for interviews and exams if I spend my time reading fiction? I thought.

'I will, in my holidays,' I replied gently.

He got up. I got up as well in a hurry. The plastic chair I sat on fell down. 'Oops,' I said.

'Easy,' he smiled.

He shook hands and said, 'The third table from here, you can meet our HR. You have cleared the technical round.'

God, you are the greatest, I thought. 'Thanks, Akash Sir,' I was so happy.

'You call me Sir again, you won't get your appointment letter,' he pulled my leg.

'Okay. I am out of here before I have to call you anything again,' I shook hands again and moved towards the third table.

HR was represented by a slightly plump lady in a coat, white shirt and grey skirt. She smiled at me and introduced herself as Mrs Fareeda and made me feel comfortable. She congratulated me for clearing the technical round.

To start off with, she asked me a few HR questions but really didn't dig deep. She then explained to me how fresher-recruitment takes place, the training program we go through to get specialized, and the level we would be absorbed in and all that was relevant.

I was issued an offer letter with the joining date, tempting figures and the clauses, which if I failed to match at the time of recruitment would render the offer letter null and void.

I was very happy to have made it, but was pretty amused to read through the Terms and Conditions. But letter in hand, I walked out of our auditorium.

I had no plans of attending the second interview of the day. I had chosen to attend my second interview the next day. The reason behind this was to give myself some time if, for some reason, I messed up big time on day one.

Manish stood there with an offer letter in his hand as well.

'Hey Manish! So, US or job?' I asked.

'The offer letter is for my confidence and the US for my dad's happiness,' he said.

'Hmm. I made it as well,' and I showed him the papers.

'You had a doubt?' he asked.

'Of course, you never know,' I said. 'Anyway, mission accomplished! Now we have to clear our finals,' I thought ahead aloud.

'Where are we celebrating?' Manish asked.

'I have a plan,' I said.

'And that is?'

'How about we give Riya a surprise welcome back party? It would be just the two of us and her?' I was all excited. I was more thrilled about getting Riya back than getting the job.

'Sounds good to me! I'll choose the place. I will meet you at 6:00 p.m. in Café Paradise. Call in Riya at 6:30. I'll order a cake on the way back now and ask them to keep it ready.' Manish was definitely a happy guy today.

'Done.' I gave him a hi-five.

I was really looking forward to celebrating with Riya. She needed to have some good times now. She had called me late last night and told me what happened after she went home from my place.

Her dad had opened the door for a change, much to Riya's shock. As she went in he said he wanted to talk to her. Riya was nervous. She didn't know what was in store, as her dad had asked specifically to talk to her only a very few times until now, and most of those memories were not happy ones.

He had put his arm around her shoulders and taken her to the lawn. Then as they sat down on the lawn chairs, she said he asked her, 'What happened to your face? Ana mausi called me to say that you have been upset lately, and now your face is bruised.'

Riya had replied, 'Nothing Dad, just a small accident. I am not upset. I am not sure why Ana mausi said that.'

Her father, going straight to the heart of the matter, had said, 'Riya, you know how much Ana loves you. She can sense any change in you. She also knows what kind of issues to bring to my notice. Let us stop beating around the bush. What is bothering you? Boy trouble?' He hit the nail right on the head, said Riya ruefully.

She had uneasily replied, 'Dad, I am not comfortable talking about it.'

'But why?' he had asked.

At which point, she said, she had burst out with her years of pent-up resentment

'Dad, you have never known what I want. Even when you know, you pretend it is not important.'

Her father was shocked, she said. He had replied astounded, 'What are you saying? I have got you everything you want! Tell me if you need anything more. I am doing all this for you.'

'Dad. Stop it!' Riya had yelled, 'Don't ever say you do everything for me. First, you need to understand what I really want and need. Why do you think all I would need is a new couch, a new TV, music system, smart phones, a new gym, a new car? Can you ever think beyond all these? '

Her father, she said, was baffled and said, 'Riya, please stop talking in riddles. Come to the point. Who is this boy?'

'The problem is not the boy, Dad. I can handle a thousand such issues. The problem is here. In this house. In our family,' Riya had said.

'Riya...' her dad had barely begun talking when she said she felt compelled to interrupt him, 'Dad, you have to listen. I am not done. I am talking like a person and not like a spoilt brat. So please cooperate. Have you ever thought I may need Mom around? Okay, I understand you both don't get along. But can't you pack up your differences for a while and behave like sane people, at least when she comes down. Your egos seem to multiply with time. Can I never see my dad and mom under the same roof?

'Okey, forget Mom, let us talk about me. Do you remember the last time we spoke face to face? Have you ever taken me for a walk? Have you realized what I need the most is your company? Have you ever picked me up from college?'

She said her dad quietly let her talk. She knew he was feeling bad, but she had to say her piece—matters that had been simmering for years had now come to a boil, thanks to Vidit, she said.

She poured out her heart, 'Dad, I need a life. A life I desire. A life that is close to reality. A life that makes me realize my existence. I am tired of all the glamour and fake masked society. Dad, I want you to trust me and my future choices. I want you to be involved with me. I expect you to at least sit with me for five minutes in a day and talk to me. Be by my side in my weak moments, when I need you, rather than your answering machine.' And then, she said, she stormed out of there.

Come to think of it, poor Ray Uncle also probably needed cheering up. Complicated families were, well...complicated!

Voices

I reached Café Paradise around 5:50 p.m. I was expecting Riya to be there by 6:30 as planned. She had no clue about the surprise party or that Manish would be there. All she knew was that I wanted to treat her for getting an offer letter from my dream company.

Manish called as I was entering the café to let me know that he was running late by ten minutes. I walked up to the counter to check if the cake was ready. It was and looked yummy.

I gave the waiter a few basic instructions as per our plan. He looked like a college boy who worked there after hours to make some pocket money, or perhaps was earning to meet some of his needs. He spoke fluent English and replied with a smile every time I spoke.

I sat at the table Manish had reserved. The café had light brown walls and the couches were coffee brown in colour. Every table had a beautiful light brown carpet with dark brown streaks underneath. Each table set was separated by light brown partitions four feet above ground which gave sufficient privacy. The whole setting made the place look like a perfect café.

There was soft music in the background. I softly hummed the verses from Lady Antebellum's song that was playing.

Picture perfect memories,
Scattered all around the floor,
Reaching for the phone cause I can't fight it any more.
And I wonder if I ever cross your mind,
For me it happens all the time.

I had to kill time. I took out a tissue and started drawing something close to a caricature of me, Riya and Manish.

As I sat smiling at the disastrous effort of drawing a caricature, I heard a very familiar voice from the next cubicle in front of me, towards the inner end of the café. It was Rajeev Uncle, Aadi's dad.

I placed the tissues back, got up and quickly checked if I was presentably dressed. I wore a red sheath top over blue jeans.

Good. I still look like I belong to this planet, I thought. *What should I say to him? How do I wish him? 'Hi Uncle! I heard your voice. So I thought I would come over and wish you.' Oops! What if he thinks I am an eavesdropping pest? No! That could be bad. Oh God! What do I say without sounding stupid?*

The interview I had faced earlier that day was far easier than deciding what should be the opening conversation with Aadi's dad. Especially when Aadi was not around to save me if I goofed up.

Should I shake hands or say, 'Namaste Uncle?'

By the time I decided what the best way to approach him was, I heard him say, 'I am worried about Aadi, Niharika. The gap between us is growing as the years pass. It is getting close to five years now since his mom passed away. He has changed a lot. He does not really open up these days,' he sighed.

I dropped the idea of popping over. This was definitely not the time to interrupt them.

'I thought things were looking better now. He gave you this watch recently. Didn't he, Rajeev?' the lady spoke.

'Yeah. He did. But that's it. I know how close we were before. He has changed a lot these days.' He sounded worried and stressed the same point over and over again.

'You have to understand he is growing up, Rajeev. Kids tend to become independent as they grow up. You can't expect him to stay the same.'

'No, that is not the point, Niharika. I know that as well. I have been there and done that. But he becomes very uncomfortable in my presence. It is like he is hiding something,' Rajeev Uncle said.

'Is he seeing someone? Do you think he wants to talk to you about it?' The lady sounded like she was smiling.

'I don't know. I do know he is very close to one girl. Her name is Saachi. She is a very good child. I like her.'

'You know what, Niharika. I have not gone into his room maybe for three years now.'

'Why?' she asked.

'I don't know. When he is in his room and I knock, he comes out and closes the door behind him. When he is not there at home, he keeps it locked. Not that I am curious or something. But why would he want to keep me away? I feel like an outsider in my own house.' Uncle sounded somewhat sad.

'Mistake, Rajeev! Don't feel bad if I point out something. What makes you say "my" own house? Isn't it his house too? You should be saying "our" house.' Ah! A woman's touch to the conversation.

'You know I don't mean it. Slip of the tongue.'

'Rajeev, when Jeeva was alive, did she talk to you about him being aloof or being reclusive about his stuff?'

'No. In fact, I remember many a time when they both sat in his room playing scrabble or carom. His mom was his best friend. There were many times when they both giggled to themselves at the dinner table.' His voice was heavy as he spoke about his late wife.

It was an emotional moment. On the one hand, Aadi spoke about having an issue with his dad. From what I could hear, it felt like Aadi was punishing him for some unknown reason. It was a riddle. But yeah, I was happy that Uncle loved him so much.

His father continued on a more cheerful note, 'Guess what! Like son, like dad. I had to uncover the hidden secrets behind that door. I made a pretext that my system had crashed and that I had to send some urgent mails. I entered his room looking for his laptop before he could fetch it out for me.' He chuckled fondly at the memory. I realized where Aadi got his naughty voice from.

Aadi would sound like his dad many years down the lane. They both had the same mischievous tone when they spoke of exciting things.

'He has a life-sized picture of Saachi on a wall bang opposite his bed,' he said happily. 'I spoke casually to him. "Nice picture, son," I said. "So, anything I need to know?" He only said that he was not very comfortable talking about such personal stuff. I tried to read his face to see what was behind the picture. But all I could sense was his anger.' Rajeev Uncle's voice sounded bewildered again.

I was dizzy all of a sudden. *What was I hearing? Aadi has my LIFE-SIZED picture in his room? I never knew that. Why was Aadi angry when Uncle asked him the question? He could have clearly stated we are friends. At least, that is what he's been telling me.*

I slid further down the couch. Now it was all the more important for Rajeev Uncle not to realize I was there.

'Why was he angry?' Niharika asked. 'Is he short-tempered?'

'No, no. He is a very gentle boy. He has very good control over his temper. In fact, I sometimes feel he has always been more mature than his age,' Rajeev Uncle said.

'Then you just be happy about it and don't worry. I think he knows what he is doing.' Her voice was cheerful.

'Okay. Forget about me. You tell me has Vishesh bothered you lately? Did he get drunk and call you again?' Uncle asked.

'No. Not after that day. All his life he wanted to divorce me. Now that we are divorced he doesn't know how to get over it.' She sounded worried.

'You are lucky you don't have children out of that marriage. Else, it would have been a bigger problem,' Uncle said.

'You are right, Rajeev. He would beat me up every time some topic about children came up. He said I was not fit to even give him a baby,' she sounded all choked up. *Poor lady, lousy man!* I fumed.

I heard Rajeev Uncle push the table and I sensed he was sitting beside her now.

'Forget it, Niharika. How long will you think about it? It's over. I am happy you had the guts to walk out of it.'

'What would I have done without you?' She seemed to calm down.

'You don't even have to think that way as I will always be there for you,' he said. 'Shall we make a move now?'

'Sure. When do you plan to come home?' she asked.

'I am sorry. I don't mean to avoid coming over. I know you have been inviting me for the last two years. My bad. But I will definitely come. I will get Aadi as well. Maybe for dinner some day, while he is here. He is always busy though. He goes out to meet his friends a lot when he comes down.' I heard them get up.

I quickly grabbed a magazine and covered my face. They passed by and did not notice me.

I heard them speak as they passed my table.

'How is your work at the NGO coming along?' Uncle questioned.

'I love it. It is very fulfilling,' Niharika said.

I lowered the magazine slightly and peeked to catch a glimpse of the lady. She was noticeably shorter than Rajeev Uncle. She looked like she was in her fifties. However, she had maintained a good physique. She had long hair that flowed down her back. She was neatly dressed in a cotton kurti and trousers. Her hair was tied back with a scarf and a smart pair of sunglasses sat perched on her nose.

Just as I was trying to recover from my eavesdropping, Manish walked in. It was 6:10.

'Hi, pretty lady,' he greeted.

'Hi buddy. Do you want me to say that you are looking good too?'

'Naah. Please don't state the obvious.' He grinned like a monkey.

Manish looked good in a military green well fitting T-shirt and cargo pants. His short sleeves showed off his muscles. He had spiked his hair and it looked good on him.

'You alright?' he asked.

'Yeah, yeah!' I said.

'No. You don't seem alright. What's up?' he asked.

'Nothing important. Forget it. I liked the cake you ordered.' I changed the topic. I myself was not sure how to interpret what I had heard. What would I tell him?

'Thanks. She should be here any minute.' He looked at his watch, all excited. It had been really long since the three of us had hung out together. The waiter had been told to dim the lights and get the candlelit cake five minutes after Riya had joined us.

'So...Manish, are you going to try to win her back?' I asked, as I sipped some water. My mind was wandering and had not yet digested what I had heard some time back, but I did my best to be in the present.

'What? Nooo. Why did you even think that?' Manish exclaimed.

'You always liked her, didn't you?' I stated the obvious.

'I like her even now. But no.' He said.

'Is it because she has been with Vidit?' I asked.

'What has that got to do with it? She knows it is a mistake now, and I am very happy she is out of it. I would accept Riya even if she had a dozen children with Vidit. You know how much I like her,' he said.

'Then, what is the problem?' I couldn't understand this.

'There is no new problem. It is the same problem as before. She always treated me like a good friend. It is good for me to accept that and be there for her. Relations don't last if they are not mutual. As a couple both parties should be eager to make it work and put in a lot of love and patience. That will happen only when you are inclined towards the person and you share a mutual chemistry.' His voice sounded deep and intense. It made me realize how much he meant what he said.

I didn't speak. I only listened.

'I want to experience love, Saachi. I want to experience magic. I want to see the person drawn to me. I want to experience the craziness,' he said.

His words seemed to push me into another world. It was magical. I felt all that for Aadi. I was drawn to him. I was crazy about everything he did and said. The chemistry between us was great. In fact, Manish had told me many times that our faces glowed when we talked to each other. I had, of course, dismissed it and said he was imagining things. I loved the warmth I felt for Aadi, and the warmth with which he treated me. I loved the way he stroked my face when I was low. I loved the way he meddled with my hair. I loved it when we held hands and watched movies together. I loved it when he looked into my eyes. I loved it when he would let me cry in his arms. I loved his dimples when he smiled. God! I was in love with Aadi!!

∾

'Saachi!' I dimly heard a voice call out my name.

'Saachi dear.' It was Manish waving a hand in front of my face. I was so lost in my thoughts that his voice sounded far away.

'Yeah, yeah!' I struggled to compose myself in the face of this new and rather disturbing realization.

'Wakey, wakey!' he carolled.

'So cheesy!' I said, and excused myself to go to the restroom. I had to be alone for some time. I wanted two minutes to think. Else, I would give away too much, and Manish would feel out of place sitting in front of me.

I stood in front of the mirror in the restroom.

What do I do? I thought. At some level I guess I had known for some time now that I loved Aadi. But I had never really said it aloud, even to myself, as I knew there was no use. What I had experienced a few days back was just plain physical attraction. But now it looked like I was moving to the next level emotionally. I was not sure if it was the right thing to do. Everything would change if Aadi sensed the change. He would feel awkward. Mostly, he'd treated me as just one of the boys, and he'd said as much fairly often. How could he be in love with me?

Then why does he have a picture of me in his bedroom? Maybe because he thought I was his best friend. He has many friends. Why mine? My heart seemed to find logic. *Maybe because he finds you photogenic.* Whatever that meant! It seemed like my mind argued for the sake of it. *But what about what Uncle said?* my heart insisted. *Exactly! He said he got angry when Uncle asked the question. What does that mean? That means he doesn't like such questions because he doesn't feel that way.* Mind dominated.

How does that matter? What matters is how you feel about him? Get a grip, girl. You will lose him if you act funny, my mind warned.

My cell rang. I jumped at the sound and my phone slipped out of my hand and fell on the floor.

I picked it up. It was a recorded message from the service provider. I shut it.

Since the time I entered the cafe until this moment now felt like the longest forty minutes of my life, which had also changed something in me. I didn't know what.

I walked out of the restroom. I expected Manish to yell at me because I had stayed there for really long. It was 6:35 p.m.

I walked towards the table and saw Manish and Riya hugging each other and Riya weeping on his shoulder.

I ran towards them and hugged them both. I didn't want to miss it for anything in the world.

'I am so sorry, guys,' Riya said, in between sobs. Her eyes looked better than the previous day.

'Don't be,' said Manish, gently wiping her tears.

'It is a human birthright to make mistakes,' I said as I sat back.

The waiter dimmed the lights. Riya looked up with some tears still glimmering in her eyes. 'Why did he dim the lights?'

The waiter walked in with the candlelit cake. Slow instrumental music played in the background. He placed it in front of Riya.

'What? I mean, why? I mean, what? Who?' She was overwhelmed.

'Happy Homecoming!' We clapped.

'Ohhh!' she wept again.

'What? You didn't like the cake? Okay, we'll eat it. Don't cry,' Manish pulled her leg.

I laughed loudly as Riya pinched Manish's arm.

'Ouch! I had forgotten what it was to be pinched by you,' Manish yelled.

'Shut up!' said Riya, and cut the cake, and we enjoyed every bite of it thoroughly. The cake was tasty enough for the fight between my heart and mind to cease for a while.

We ordered grilled sandwiches and some coke. Riya spoke as we ate.

'Guys. Thanks for all the plots you set up to irritate Vidit and me. I have a master plan now to end it with him. I need your help for that.' She sounded excited.

'Yeah! We are all ears,' I said.

'Aye, aye, captain,' Manish raised his hand.

Riya let us into the plot she had woven to teach Vidit a lesson. The plot seemed to belong to the umpteen number of Bollywood movies Riya watched.

'Good one, Riya,' Manish and I exclaimed when she finished telling us what it was. We were more than ready to stand by her side. This was no time to tell her what a drama queen she was. But, in a way, she was right. Vidit was a tough nut to crack and this plan would make him spill the beans.

We sat there for the next one hour and caught up on everything we had missed during the separation.

'So, how is Aadi?' Riya asked.

My mind went back to what I had overheard. I wanted to tell them both. However, I decided against it. Instead, I stuck to, 'He is fine.' I told Riya about his designing skills having turned into a business, along with his studies.

'Good on him.' Riya was excited. 'I am going to ask him for a treat as well. He better take me to Royal Gardenia. I hope you don't mind, Saachi,' she winked.

'Of course you should ask him for a treat, why would I mind?' I said.

'Come on, Saachi. How long will you guys beat around the bush? You are so in love with each other. Any idiot can make out what is between you both. You both are made for each other. You guys are on fire. Accept it.'

'Aadi is as good a friend to me, as Manish is. I have told you this a million times, but you find it fun to link us up.' I knew I was lying. There was only so much I could say. I loved Aadi, every bit of him. I loved him for the fun he was. I loved him for the heart he had. I loved the way he felt for others. I loved the way he twisted his brows. I loved all the hairstyles he tried out to look cool. I felt secure and wanted every time he held me. I loved the volumes his eyes spoke. I loved him for all his flaws. But I also respected the fact that he was not looking for a relationship.

'What? You feel the same about Aadi the way you feel for Manish?' Riya dragged every word in that sentence.

'He he. That is the biggest joke,' Manish laughed.

'Guys! Can we stop this here? Let's leave Aadi out of this and have a good time.' I tried to smile.

We spoke for the next half an hour of where we would all be a year from now. All our plans and dreams that we treasured.

Manish volunteered to drop Riya back, and I left on my own on my black stallion, as I lovingly imagined my little Scooty to be. My mind whirled with all the voices in my head. That night I slept at 3:00 a.m. I was unable to shut down. My life had changed forever. It had dawned on me that I was in love. There was an acceptance. They say your first love will live with you and die with you. Aadi's title had changed from a 'special friend' to 'the love of my life'.

Riya had an eventful evening as well. After she reached home she called her mom that night and said she wanted to talk. Her mom, she said, wanted to call her back because she was going out with friends, 'but I said Mom, no. Stay back. I have to talk to you.' She narrated what happened next.

'What happened, dear?' Riya's mother asked her, 'What is so urgent? Can't we do this later? I can't cancel on my friends.'

'Mom, I called to say I am sorry.'

There was silence on the other side, recalled Riya. She asked, 'Mom, you there?'

'Yes,' her mother replied.

'Mom, I also called to say I love you and I am missing you.'

She heard her mom's cell buzz. Her mother picked it up and quickly informed her caller that something very important had just come up, and she could not make it. Then she returned to Riya's call, 'Baby, what's up?'

'Mom,' Riya wept.

'Don't cry, Riya. You are a strong girl. What happened? Was your dad rude to you?' she asked.

'Mom, why do you think anything that goes wrong with me should be because of Dad. No, he was not rude to me.'

'Oh! It is just that your dad...never mind, Riya. What is bothering you?'

'Mom, I am crying because all that was bothering me is no more bothering me. It is my moment of realization...'

'Child, things sound complicated,' her mother said gently, 'Go to sleep. It is late in India. We can talk tomorrow.'

'No, Mom. I want to talk today, now. I am sorry if I have hurt you all these years. You must understand I was not mature enough to understand adult relationships. It must have been very tough for you. I complicated your life even more. I want to make up for all those years. I want to join you in London. I want you to help me become a fashion designer. I want you to retire. I want to take care of you.'

Her mom sobbed on the other end.

'Mom. Please don't cry.'

'No, I won't. Ana always told me that I had given birth to an angel. It is so true. Thanks, honey, for being so good at heart. I will come down and talk to your dad. This time, without arguing, we will do it like adults. He should understand. Now you are big enough to choose what you want to do with your life. I will guard you and be with you like a shadow.'

'Oh! Mom, I love you.'

Roller-Coaster Ride

My phone buzzed to wake me up at 7:30 a.m. Aadi's name flashed. I was nervous about taking his call.

'Hi sweetheart! Good morning,' Aadi said on the other end.

'Hi...hi,' I blabbered.

'How was your evening? I thought you would leave a message or call. You didn't do either,' Aadi said.

I was in no state to call him the previous night. I didn't know what I would say.

'I didn't want to disturb you,' I said.

'Since when did your calls start disturbing me? You know I can live and die talking to you.' He was his usual playful self.

'Hmm,' is all I could say. All of a sudden everything he said had started affecting me. This was not the first time he had said such stuff though.

'What's wrong, Saachi?' It was tough to hide anything from Aadi, and I would have to do it for the rest of my life now. I didn't know how.

'Nothing in particular. I slept really late,' I said.

'Wow. Why? I know you can abandon the world for your sleep. How come you missed your sleep?' Aadi was curious to know what was on my mind.

'I guess it is the interviews, the end of college, friends moving in separate directions, too many changes in the coming few days. I am not ready for it, I guess!' I made up. It was not completely a lie though.

'I understand,' he said. 'Don't worry about it. Just take one day at a time. We will see how it goes. Now get your butt off that bed and get ready for the day's interview. I will wait for your call. By the way, I am meeting Mahi for lunch today,' he said, before he hung up.

I landed on Mother Earth with a thump. I was no more floating in air. Long-distance relations are tough, especially with beautiful 'adventurous' girls like Mahi around. Any little hope of looking at our relationship seriously just vanished. His last sentence nixed everything.

The day's interview was easier than the first day's. I was very tired at the end of it, as I had watched every stroke of the clock until 3:00 a.m. the might before and all I wanted to do was hit the bed as soon as I got back home.

It was 1:00 p.m. as I wound up and walked with the second offer letter in my hand. I made it a point to meet Prof. Sharada before I left the campus. She was my mentor and for some reason I was her favourite. She was happy to know that I had bagged both the offers. She wished me luck for the exams which were to start in a month and said she was very proud of me.

I was to call Aadi. I looked at my watch. It was 1:20 p.m. Right now, he must be having lunch with Mahi, I thought, and for the first time, I felt terribly jealous and uncomfortable. I didn't know if I wanted to call him. But then I decided to call him as I had to learn to digest the truth as well. There was no use running away from it.

I rang him up. For some reason he did not receive the call. *What is keeping him so busy?* I thought. I called again.

'Hello,' a female voice spoke.

My hands and feet went cold even though it was 30 degrees centigrade in the open where I stood.

'Hi,' I said hesitantly. I knew it was Mahi. *Why was she on the phone? Why didn't Aadi take my call? What would she say now?* My mind was shooting too many questions at a time.

'Hi Saachi!' she literally screamed into the speaker. She seemed to be 'unnecessarily' excited!

My eyes widened. Thank God she could not see me. 'Hi. Who is this?' I said.

'It's Mahi. Aadi's friend. Hi Saachi! I am so happy to hear your voice,' she said. The background was noisy. It looked like they were at some very busy eat-out.

'Likewise,' I was diplomatic. I was just about to ask for Aadi while Mahi burst out uncontrollably.

'I have heard so much about you. Aadi talks about you all the time. Saachi this, Saachi that. I always wanted to talk to you,' she chirped.

'Oh!' is all I said. It didn't mean anything. It is obvious you talk about a person when you know someone for so many years. That didn't clear any of my questions about the two of them.

'Where is Aadi? Can I talk to him please?' I asked.

'He is actually not here.' She paused uncomfortably. 'Well, it is kind of my fault.' She chuckled then.

What is it that you did? I am sure it is your fault. I was eager to know what was happening 850 kilometres away in Pune.

'I saw a man go by with some strawberries. You see, I love strawberries. I just happened to tell Aadi that. He is such a sweet guy. He ran across the lane trying to catch up with him. Looks like he'll be back only when he buys some strawberries.' She sounded dreamy.

You squeaky-voiced-brainless-adventurous-cheesy-strawberry-loving bimbo, I cursed in my mind. For some reason I imagined a strawberry in her mouth, and Aadi wanting to grab it right from her mouth with his hands all over her. I was going crazy.

'Hello. You there?' Her voice seemed extra squeaky now. Actually, her voice was fine. It was my mind which was playing games. Why was I on this call? Why was I wasting my time talking to her just to mess up my brain?

'Yeah...yeah,' I said, trying to sound fine.

'Any message for him?' she asked.

What the hell! How dare you take a message for him? Do you even know whom you are talking to, my heart screamed. *Saachi, you are being unreasonable,* my mind tried to bring me to my senses. Isn't it the most obvious thing anyone would do when the intended person is not around? She was trying to be nice and here I was judging her.

'Yeah, sure. Please tell him I got through my second interview as well,' I said.

'Great! I will take a treat from him on your behalf,' she said, as she cut the call.

Go ahead, lady! He is all yours. Maybe you should meet him for dinner as well. Why don't you wear a tank-top with strawberries all over it and dance with him just to celebrate my success? I was unimaginably angry as I slid my phone into my sling bag, kick-started my bike and left the place.

What is wrong with me? I thought. *Am I going to get my periods? No, that's a fortnight away. Not so quick. Why am I behaving this way?* I thought. I was very irritated.

Ideally, it was supposed to be a happy day as I had two offer letters in my hand, and it was what I had aimed for. This was not happening.

The roads seemed to be crowded today. I usually enjoyed my bike rides, but today, I felt people were acting crazy on the road. The public was its usual nonsensical self, but I guess I was intolerant. We Bengalurians are very tolerant people. We think power cuts, bad roads, traffic, smoke, dug-up drains, the world's tallest bumps, no water supply are all sent to this city just to make us the most tolerant people ever to exist on this globe.

I looked around at the orderly chaos. Orderly because these things never change! A man crossing the road, his head bent and his hands in his pockets, very similar to people strolling on their own private balcony; an indecisive middle-aged lady running to the middle of the road, and then running backwards to the footpath because she failed to cross the road; a teenage girl talking on her mobile, with a hand held out to freeze the fast moving vehicles as she crossed the road.

I drove through all of that madness with a hot, boiling pot of jealousy bubbling inside me, and made it home. I saw a Civic parked outside my house. Great! The last thing I wanted do was to meet guests. I would have to pretend to be happy to see them now, when all I wanted to do was snore away to glory! Sleep is the best way to get over the worst of any situation.

A bed! A bed! My kingdom for a bed! my mind screamed.

I figured one of my relatives would have bought a Civic and would have come to brag about their new possession. That is what relatives are meant to do. Turn up when you least expect them, and go missing when you need them the most.

I parked my bike and walked in. I looked haggard due to lack of sleep. I could hear laughter filling the living-room. I saw an elderly looking man sitting with my dad. There was another person sitting with them with his back to the main door.

My parents smiled as soon as I walked in.

'Saachi! Come. Look who is here?' My dad made me sit beside him. I saw a neatly dressed young man, slightly older to me, sitting right opposite. I can't say he was handsome, but yes, he was definitely charming.

'Meet my childhood friend Keshav. He lived in Chennai all this while. They have just now moved back to Bengaluru. We happened to bump into each other,' my dad introduced his friend.

'Saachi is all grown up and looks beautiful,' Keshav Uncle remarked kindly, adding, 'Meet my son Madhav. He is working in California. He is here for his cousin's wedding.' I smiled at Keshav and he smiled back. We exchanged a brief 'Hi'.

'Saachi, why don't you show him around the house? Madhav is getting bored,' my dad said.

'Okay,' I said. I had to be polite. They were guests. Guests are God and if God got angry, I would be in big trouble.

I looked at my mom and she seemed to be smiling from ear to ear. *Why is she so happy?* I thought.

I completed the formality of showing Madhav around the house. He had curly hair and wore black framed glasses. He worked as a finance consultant in one of the firms in San Francisco, so I gathered.

He entered my room and didn't seem to budge from there. Maybe he didn't want to be in the hall and hear all the flashback stories which both our fathers were thoroughly enjoying.

'Your room is beautiful,' Madhav said.

My phone rang. It was Aadi. I didn't pick up the call. It was the first time I had ever done that, yeah, unless I was in the bathroom when he had called.

'I think you are getting a call,' Madhav said.

'Yeah, it's my friend. I'll call back later,' I said.

'You want me to leave?' he asked politely.

'No...no. Stay. It's okay. Not an important call,' I said. Aadi's call at any point was more than important to me. But he had to wait. He had made me wait as he had gone strawberry hunting! The most important task he had on hand! I could imagine that he had run with such enthusiasm to please the hot chick that he had left his phone behind. Aadi would never leave his phone behind! I always teased him that he was married to it. He was dangerously possessive about it.

Madhav cleared his throat to get my attention.

'Sorry, you were saying?' I said.

'I said you have a beautiful room,' he repeated.

Really?! I thought. I looked around. There was a collage of my pictures from childhood till my latest pics. It had been put together as a gift by Manish and Riya for my last birthday. There was a study table beside the window on which my laptop was placed, and I had displayed all the mementoes I had received on the upper shelf.

My bed was neatly made and my curtains seemed to blend with the wall colour. There was a couch beside the bed. I had a laundry bag which read 'Feel free to dump'. There was a dressing table at the corner with the least number of cosmetics a girl could ever possess.

Yeah! Not a bad job, I told myself.

'Thanks,' I said.

He walked up to the collage and said, 'You look really good in these pics.'

'Thanks,' I repeated.

My phone rang again. This time I picked it up. I didn't let Aadi talk. 'I'll call you back in the evening. I am busy now,' I finished my sentence and hung up even before he could open his mouth.

Serves the strawberry king right. I knew I was being mean. I could have excused myself and taken his call. But I didn't.

Madhav sat on the couch beside my bed. I had no choice but to say, 'Make yourself comfortable.'

He chatted for the next ten minutes. I felt he was a nice guy. If not for my lousy mood. I would have been very happy to have met him.

'Saachi,' I heard my mom call.

I went into the kitchen. My mom had placed some pakodas and coffee on a plate. She asked me to give it to Madhav. As I was walking out she caught my hand and kissed my cheek.

'Mom, you are weird today,' I said, as I walked out.

Madhav and I spoke until they had to leave and it was a very casual conversation. He said he would send me a Friend request on Facebook.

I told my parents I wanted to sleep and went to my room as they continued to chat in excitement. For some reason I put off my phone before I went to sleep.

I slept like a pig which had hogged more than it could digest. I woke up to the noise of my mom knocking persistently on my door.

'Saachi. Get up! Aadi has called three times now. He wants to talk to you,' my mom literally screamed. She hated it when I locked my room as waking me up was not an easy task, especially when you had no access to the room.

Aadi had called the landline as my phone was switched off. The first two times he had asked my mom to let me sleep, but the third time he wanted to talk.

I took the call. 'Aadi. I was sleeping,' I said, with my eyes half open.

'Do you know what time it is?' His voice was impatient.

I opened my eyes with great difficulty and looked at the watch. It was 7:30 p.m.

'Wow. It's 7:30. I have slept for more than four hours,' I said.

'Yes. Have you ever seen a girl sleep this long in the afternoon?' he asked.

'I am not a girl,' I said.

'Yeah! That's a different story,' he said. 'Why didn't you take my call in the afternoon?' He was annoyed.

'I was talking to Madhav.' I adjusted my hair with one hand and adjusted my crumpled skirt with the other.

'Who Madhav?' he asked.

'My father's long-lost friend's son who has come down from the US,' I said.

'Why did he come?' Aadi sounded serious.

'What do you mean?' I said. 'They just came to meet my dad.' Aadi was lucky I was in a sleepy mood. If I had been in the mood I was in before I went to sleep, he would have been in trouble.

I can't talk to Madhav while he is busy feeding strawberries to Mahi? What a joke, I thought.

'Are you sure?' Aadi asked.

'Sure of what, Aadi?' I was being patient.

'Sure that they just came to meet your dad?' he asked again. He was unusually jumpy today.

'Aadi, why are you asking so many questions? I am done with all my interviews and answering questions, and I am not going to answer any more questions.'

'Sorry. I don't know why I am asking these questions as well. It is just that I felt bad when you didn't answer my call and your phone was switched off. You never do that. I am still waiting to know how you fared in your interview,' he said.

'Really! Now you want to know! Do you know how I felt when you had left your phone behind to buy strawberries on the road when you knew I would call?' I burst out. I couldn't hold it anymore.

'Strawberries? What strawberries?' he said.

'Stop acting innocent, Aadi.' I was upset. 'How long will you hide from me that you are seeing Mahi? I thought I was your best friend and you tell me everything.' I banged the phone.

I was in tears. Luckily, my mom was not around.

The landline buzzed again. It was Aadi, without doubt.

'What are you talking, Saachi? I am lost. I think you were dreaming. Baby, wake up. It's Aadi here.' He tried to make me feel better.

'Yeah! I guess I had a nightmare. Forget it. Tell me why you called?' I asked between angry sobs.

'Saachi, why are you crying? Buddy, what is wrong? When did you call? I didn't have a missed call. And what strawberries are you talking about? You know I don't like strawberries. Why would I go to buy them?' He fired more questions than I could try to remember, if I had to answer them all.

'Yeah! Someone else likes strawberries,' was all that I said.

'Who likes strawberries?' he asked.

I narrated the whole conversation that took place earlier that afternoon. Aadi had never seen me angry before. I was very angry as I felt he was trying to hide stuff from me. *I never hide anything. Why should he? All I asked for was some honesty.*

'What? Is that what happened? Weird. Why would she say that?' His voice was very faint and he was badly surprised. 'Give me a minute. I will call you back.' He hung up before I said anything.

I ran back to the room, switched on my mobile and called him back. His line was busy. I tried for the next ten minutes. It was busy again. I gave up. I decided to wait for his call in spite of my restlessness. I washed my face and brushed my teeth to kill time. The phone rang again as I wiped my face.

'Hello Aadi. Why did you hang up?'

'I am sorry, Saachi,' Aadi sounded low.

'Aadi, sorry for what?' I was anxious. I didn't know what to say.

'Well, I called Mahi. She played the innocent and denied the whole thing. But when I raised my voice she told me the truth. I had stepped out to freshen up and had left the phone behind by mistake.' He paused.

'But why would she make up such a story?' I asked.

'She thinks she loves me, you moron, that is why. She told me when I confronted her just now. She was jealous of you, as I always talk of you and come to meet you even when my group of friends here make plans to visit some place or the other. She thought that I was in love with you,' he said.

Every word of his rang like a hammer in my ears. I was silent. I didn't speak.

'Hello. You there?' he asked.

'Yeah! I am happy for you, Aadi,' I said.

'Happy? For what? No…no…you got it all wrong. Of course I don't love her, Saachi. You know me. I should have picked up the signs. Every time she knew I was coming down to Bengaluru she would stop me and invite me for something or the other every weekend. I just thought she was trying to have fun, like the rest of us. When we went out for the movies, I now realize she always sat beside me even though we were in a gang,' he was thinking aloud.

'Anyway, sorry for all the confusion, Saachi. You didn't deserve to go through it. By the way, was madam jealous that I went out to buy strawberries?'

So he didn't love her. But he had made it clear that he didn't love me as well.

'Yeah. What will you do about it?'

'Nothing. I feel good,' he laughed.

'And why is that?' I asked.

'Because you are showing signs of turning into a girl. Otherwise, you are so much on guard always.' He laughed again. It was truly difficult to understand him.

We spoke for the next ten minutes or so. I told him about the interview and Riya's plan to teach Vidit a lesson. I made very sure not to utter a word about me seeing his dad in the cafe or what I had heard. He hung up saying he would log on to the net to chat by ten at night. I had slept a good number of hours and would obviously be wide awake till midnight.

That night at dinner I could sense my mom urging my dad to talk to me about something.

'Madhav is a very nice boy. What do you think, Saachi? Well-educated, well-settled,' he said.

'What is so nice about that?' I said.

'No, even otherwise he comes across as a dude,' said my father, trying to sound cool.

'He is okay,' I said. I wondered why we were even talking about him.

'He had come to meet you, Saachi,' my mom could not hold the excitement any more.

'Meet me? I thought they had come to see dad,' I spoke like a dud. 'Wait! You mean like a bridegroom thing?' I yelled as realization dawned.

Both of them giggled. Now I understood why mom was behaving weirdly that afternoon.

'Give me a break!' This was annoying.

'Relax, Saachi,' my dad said. 'They are aware of your aspirations, they know that you want to work for a couple of years, do a Masters later, and all that you have in mind. They are okay with it. In fact, Madhav was very happy to know that you have thought so much for yourself. No hurry at all. He just wants to start dating you, as you folks call it these days. Get married whenever you both are ready.' My dad tried to make it sound like a fair deal.

'What? I can't believe you both were planning to set me up. How could you? Mom! Why didn't you tell me?' I was almost in tears now. I didn't know how to react. I left the table and walked to my room.

'Saachi, wait!' My mom followed in before I could shut the door.

'Let us talk it out. You know we will never force you,' she said.

'I always thought my parents were different and they understood me. But you are like any other parents, narrow-minded, and would like to see me do exactly what you have in mind for me. You don't think I am a person by myself too. I may have some desires. Why does it have to be like that? Why don't you parents understand?' I sobbed. I knew I was being a drama queen. But drama is good sometimes.

'You know what! You people think it is your right to dictate to us just because you give birth to us. Did I ask to be born? No, I was born because you wanted to have kids. Right from when we should be born till when we should give birth is decided by you. Why?' I had rarely spoken to my mom like this. But I was irritated hearing the same stories in everyone's house, and I expected my parents to at least not join the bandwagon.

'Saachi! You know for a fact that we are not like that. It is just your anger talking. Have we ever tried to place you under house arrest or restrict anything you do? We know you are intelligent enough to handle yourself. We don't even ask where you go or what you have been up to! We have been reasonable. Even now we have not committed to anything. We wanted to check with you.'

I hugged her and cried

'Saachi, we didn't think it would hurt you so much. We are sorry,' my mom said. 'I promise you we will never do anything you don't like.'

'It's not you. I think you people just did what you felt may be good,' I said, coming back to my senses. 'It's about me,' I confessed, still hugging her.

'It's about Aadi, right?' my mom asked, like she had read my mind. 'I know you love him, Saachi. But do you think it makes sense? You know, and I know as well, that he does not believe in marriage. What's the point?' she continued.

We kids think we are smart and our parents are outdated, but there are times when they prove they have seen more life than you and I, and that they can see through without your even mentioning anything.

I was speechless. I didn't have an answer.

'Saachi, trust me. I will be the happiest to see you with Aadi. We both like Aadi a lot and he is a great boy. But it is not always easy to swim against the current. You will get tired of it,' she cajoled, as she stroked my head lovingly.

'Mom, can you do me a favour? Can you talk to Dad and give me time till I finish my exams? I am not in a position to think straight now. I need time to think,' I said.

'Sure. I think that is the best for all of us,' said my mom.

That night I logged on to the net to chat with Aadi. Madhav was quick to send me a Friend request. I accepted it. I didn't mention any of the night's events to Aadi. There was enough masala for him to digest for the day, after the incident with Mahi. I decided to wait for the right time.

Mahi had called Aadi many times later and apologized and wanted to be his friend as before, but he was not sure.

'Why are you not comfortable?' I asked. 'Is it because she told you she loves you?'

'No. Not really. It is not like the first time someone has done that. My friend Sarah, the one you saw me with in Baker's Nest, had told me she loved me in college. But till date we are friends. It does not matter. But here, Mahi lied to get rid of you. I don't think she is friend material,' he said.

He had a point. Such people can be scary.

'I thought you said you liked her because she was adventurous. Consider this as one of her adventures and forgive her,' I said, pulling his leg.

'Shut up, Saachi! You are not helping,' he yelled back.

We were on voice chat for the next two hours. We didn't realize how time flew when we spoke to each other. We shared videos, youtube fun clips, songs, everything we liked. Read reviews together. There was always a lot to do.

Goa—Bares it all

⌇

The next two months whizzed by before we could realize it. The trio of us were busy with exams, and Aadi was also busy with final semester activities.

Madhav tried to get in touch with me in more than one way. But with time he realized I was not interested in him in terms of a long-term relationship. My parents understood as well. I had decided that if Aadi could not be my life partner, I would accept it. But I was also sure that I didn't want to choose the most convenient way of settling down in life.

Riya tried to avoid Vidit as much as possible contact with him and kept it to phone calls, on the pretext of exams. Her mom had come down to stay with her. Riya's father had come to terms with the fact that his daughter could no more be caged. She had, free will and would set out in pursuit of her desires, sooner or later. It was better that she chose to stay with her mom than decide not to stay with both.

Finally, the day every engineering student dreams of arrived. We had completed our exams and were free now.

Riya would avoid talking to me and Manish in the campus when Vidit was around. We played along. Riya had little time in hand; she was aware that Vidit would grow restless if she avoided him during the holidays. She started working on her plan.

The Pereira group owned a beach resort in south Goa. Riya cajoled her dad into a Goa trip with her friends. Mr Pereira was more than happy to make arrangements as his dear daughter had lived up to his dream of completing her course.

Vidit had one uncompleted wish on his list that Riya was very well aware of. He wanted to get her into bed. It was very easy for her to talk him into a Goa stay at her own beach resort. What more could he ask for? Free stay, where he would be treated like a king, bathe in booze and sex on the beach. He was about to achieve his biggest target in life and in style. Little was he aware of what was in store for him. He should have known by now that if Riya was ready to die for him, she could even kill him!

Manish and I were to arrive at the resort a few hours before Riya and Vidit, and stay under cover. Aadi was more than happy to join us. Everything went to plan. Manish and I took the night train and reached Goa by 11:00 a.m. Aadi was already there by the time we reached the resort. He had taken a bus from Pune. He welcomed us with a hug. Riya had made sure that her chauffeur picked us up from Vasco station.

It was my first time in Goa. It was a refreshing change from the hustle and bustle of a metro city. It was a serene state with its unending landscapes. I couldn't wait to explore more of it. But we all knew, first things first.

Riya and Vidit flew down to Goa and reached Dabolim airport at 1:00 p.m. Vidit was on cloud nine when an Audi came to pick them up at the airport. There were lot of things he could brag about to his friends. He was living a life of the prince.

∽

Penthouses were kept ready for us in Wing A, while Riya and Vidit were to stay in a penthouse in Wing D. These penthouses were only reserved for Riya and her family or close friends, and never rented out.

Our penthouse on the sixth floor had four bedrooms. Each one of us took a room and Riya was to join us later, after the successful execution of her plan. The penthouse had all the modern amenities, and the best part was the terrace which overlooked the beach and had a private pool.

We took leisurely showers in bathrooms which looked better than my living-room back home. Food was sent up to the penthouse and we further discussed our plan over lunch. We were ready for Riya's signal to set out on our adventure.

Vidit was a rogue. But every rogue has a weakness. Vidit did not know how to swim! Naturally, he was afraid to go into water that was more than knee deep. Riya, on the contrary, was a fish. She loved to swim and was a regular at water sports during every holiday in Goa. She loved the water.

Vidit's agenda was all about booze and sex. At lunch he had some Goan cashew feni, as he needed the guts to go on a water scooter ride with Riya. He had to please her if he wanted her to get into bed with him for the next five days.

Riya owned sexy-looking water scooters in all available colours. We watched from the penthouse terrace as she got onto her favourite bike with Vidit hesitantly perched behind her. Riya's private beach gave them enough privacy.

We saw Riya smooch Vidit before they set off. *Wow! A kiss for a kill!* I thought.

It was a cue for us to head to the beach and set out on our water scooters which Riya had kept ready.

Aadi and I took a scooter and Manish rode another.

We could see Riya ride into the sea. We followed her on our bikes. Riya brought her scooter to a halt about 900 metres into the sea.

Aadi and Manish rode towards her. The scooters hit the waves with a thud.

I held Aadi tight. In spite of the task on hand I was very aware of our proximity. But there was no way I would let go of him. This was my first time on a water scooter. The salt water of the sea splashed us as we rode. I could feel the heat of his body.

We reached Riya and Vidit within minutes. Aadi and Manish brought their scooters to halt facing them. Vidit seemed to be seeing stars in daylight.

His voice was shaky when he screamed, 'Riya, why did you stop the scooter? What the hell are these jerks doing here?'

'They just came to say hi to us, Vidit. Relax!' Riya replied.

'What the f***? What do you mean, say hi?' He was perplexed and scared to death.

Riya got up and sat face to face with Vidit. The scooter wobbled, much to Vidit's fear.

'Riya, what are you doing? You will kill us,' he screamed.

'Nothing. I just want to know how much you love me,' Riya said.

Vidit looked at us across her shoulders. We sat as silent spectators. After all, it was Riya's show.

'What kind of madness is this? Darling, you know how much I love you,' Vidit tried smooth talk.

'How much?' Riya screamed. 'If you trust me the way I trusted you when I fell for you, then jump into the sea,' she said.

'Never! Why would I jump?' Vidit blabbered.

'Why not? I am here to pull you up, plus you have your life jacket on,' she said.

'I don't care. Riya, I will slap you if you don't start the bike,' Vidit threatened.

'Try doing it,' said Riya, as she dived into the sea and surfaced. Manish dived in as well and joined her.

'Where are you going? Come here, you bitch,' Vidit screamed. He was terribly scared to even move an inch as the waves jolted the scooter. Our presence made him all the more nervous.

'Did you call me a bitch?' Riya said.

'F*** you, Riya,' he said.

'Why not? Right here, right now. Come, join me,' she said, as she pushed the bike to the side with Manish's help and Vidit fell into the water.

Vidit sank and went 'glug, glug, glug' into the water and surfaced. He had swallowed some water. He was gasping for breath. One dip into the sea and his ego was washed out.

'Riya, I am sorry. Save me, save me,' he screamed for life. It was nice to see him beg. 'You can't leave me in the middle of nowhere. You love me, Riya. How can you do this?' he wept. I am sure by now he must have peed in his boxers.

'Really? Then how did you think that you could take me for a ride and dump me in the middle of nowhere?' Riya was uncontrollable. 'Did you think it was easy to use my love as my weakness? Who gave you the right, Vidit? When were you planning to tell me? Getting me to bed and God knows what later was in your mind.'

Vidit, by now, knew it was a waste denying any of her claims. There was a whole world of aqua underneath and he shivered every time a fish or a coral touched his body.

'What do you want me to do? I told you I am sorry,' Vidit pleaded.

'Jerk, you tell me what you will do?' Riya demanded.

Riya and Manish got back on their scooters with ease. All three of them started their scooters. Vidit knew they were capable of abandoning him in the sea.

'Wait. Stop, stop,' he screamed. At this very moment it seemed like all the mistakes of his life had dawned on him. He was standing at the doors of hell.

Vidit had realized that he would not drown with the life jacket on. But a phobia developed over twenty plus years cannot leave within minutes. The waves, the noise of the water, the vastness of the ocean, the taste of salt in his mouth, the uncertainty that came with all of it, his own guilt and helplessness about the situation were still working on his mind.

He hit the water hard with his right hand out of frustration. He screamed loudly like a mad man. He wept. He fell silent for a while.

Riya was not moved. She was very angry with him. She had stood against her friends for life, for him. She had built many dreams with him. He had fooled around and ill-treated her.

We sat silently. The scooters were shut down and were carried by the buoyancy of the water.

Riya's face was fuming. Her eyes were waiting to see what would come out of Vidit's mouth.

Vidit looked up, 'Riya…Riya,' he managed. Riya raised one of her brows. I sighed. I was losing patience.

'I apologize, Riya. To you and your friends. I apologize to all the women I have ever mistreated. I always thought girls were weak and making a fool of them was easy. Today I realize how strong a girl can be if she wants. Riya, I know I am not fit for this. But I am ready to take you into my life just the way you wanted. Without your money or without anything that comes with your family name. Please forgive me,' Vidit sobbed.

Looking into the eyes of their own fear is not everyone's cup of cake. Vidit's phobia for deep waters made him blurt out all that he wanted to and didn't want, as well.

Riya started her bike and left. She went deeper into the sea and rode faster. She had to take all the negative emotions out of her system. Manish pulled Vidit onto his scooter and patted his back. He was ashamed to look at any of us.

We drove towards the shore. Riya stayed in the sea for some time. Vidit left for the penthouse, probably to pack and find the quickest way to get from Goa to Bengaluru.

Riya fell onto the sand and wept. Manish and Aadi left for the penthouse, and I lay beside Riya looking at the sun. She gathered herself after a while.

I lay with my head resting on my arms.

'You okay?' I asked.

'Hmm…' she said.

'You want to be alone for a while? Will you be fine?'

'No, please stay,' she said.

We lay there in the sun for another fifteen minutes. Neither of us spoke. The sea looked beautiful.

I broke the silence. 'You will be fine, Riya. I know it is not easy to forget but you have got to try. Try to focus on what you want to do next. When bad things happen to good people, it just means that there is something very good in store ahead as well. Maybe Vidit came into your life for a reason. You won't realize that now. But, definitely, at some point you will. Be confident about yourself and take it easy. Trust me, your bad experience with him will help you realize how precious a relationship is when you finally find an honest one.'

'You are right,' she slowly whispered, almost like she was talking to herself.

She got up and pulled me up. She spoke to me about her plans for us that evening. She said she had planned for me, Aadi and Manish to go on a cruise where she had made bookings for our dinner, while she wanted to stay back at the resort and have some time out.

I respected her need for privacy. These are the junctures where the fight is usually between 'you' and 'you'.

We walked back to the resort. I accompanied her to her penthouse. I wanted to be sure Vidit was no more there. The resort manager was waiting for her at her door.

'Ma'am, your guest left. I was not sure it was planned that way. He even refused a ride to the bus-stand. He said he was fine. I just wanted to make sure we are good.'

'We are good, we are very good,' she smiled faintly.

She asked him to get her stuff moved to our penthouse and walked in. I followed her.

Vidit had left a note for her at the bedside.

It read, 'You are the most beautiful girl I have met. You have a heart to go with it. I will never forget the time we spent with each other. I am sorry, I messed up. Please try to forgive me—Vidit.'

She was expressionless. She moved to her window and looked out. Now that was the most sensible and decent action I had ever witnessed Vidit doing.

'Riya, won't you show me round your resort?' I tried to divert her.

'Yes, yes, sorry,' she said. She took me round the resort and introduced me to all her staff. There was a swimming pool overlooking the sea. There was a spa and a multi-cuisine bar and restaurant. There were some indoor games and a room where they taught yoga every evening. There were well kept lawns in and around, and a fountain with sculptures of dolphins.

She said she dreamt of having a chain of boutiques at all her hotels.

'God bless!' I said.

We went to the penthouse and met Aadi and Manish, who were lying on the couch like lazy pigs. It was nice to see Aadi relaxed and not up to something like he always was. He lay there bare-chested. I had never seen him that naked before. His regular work-outs were very evident.

'Hey guys!' Riya said.

'Please accept my thanks,' she said. 'I have reserved a table for the three of you on a cruise. My chauffeur will drive you down. I want you guys to have a great evening,' she said.

'You are not joining us?' both Aadi and Manish spoke at the same time.

'No. I'll skip it this time, if you don't mind. I just want to be alone for a while. I promise from tomorrow we will have a blast together. Sulking doesn't suit me,' she smiled.

'I'll drop out as well,' said Manish. 'Riya, do you have bikes for rent here? I want to visit a friend at Benalium. I may not meet him once I go abroad,' he said.

'Great! It is just the two of us then,' I said. 'We'll skip it as well and watch the sunset from the balcony and imagine we are on a cruise.'

'No, no, you should both go,' Manish said.

'We will go,' said Aadi. He nodded, indicating that Riya needed to be left alone.

'You guys have got to hurry then,' Riya said. 'It is an hour's drive to Colva Beach from here. The cruise sets out at 6:00 p.m.'

I dressed in a blue cotton Goan shirt and a wrap-around. I wore beads on my neck and took my cell in a clutch purse. Aadi wore white cotton trousers and a bright orange cotton shirt. Manish had left to meet his friend with a map in hand. Riya walked us to the entrance and bade us bye.

Aadi captured every nook and corner of Goa on the way to Colva, and in all that, every third snap he took was mine.

'Aadi, stop it. How many of those do you want?' I hit his hand.

'Enough to fill an album,' he said.

'Very funny, Aadi,' I said.

He didn't bother and he didn't stop clicking. I had only one option. I pulled strange faces, hoping he would stop. But he was amused.

'I always knew you were talented,' he chuckled.

The cruise was called 'Blue Lagoon'.

'Wow, this is neat!' Aadi exclaimed, as he jumped out of the car and opened the door for me.

᠔

We walked onto the cruise-ship and a woman dressed in Goan attire welcomed us aboard. They served a fruit punch as a welcome drink. We were showed to the deck on which tables and chairs were neatly placed and decorated with white cloth and red satin ribbons. The arrangement overlooked what looked like a dance floor. The sun was at its best red and ready to set. Everything was just perfect.

We took a corner table. Aadi asked the steward to take our pictures. We posed like a happy couple.

The cruise took off with a brief welcome speech, and the enthusiastic man on the dais tried to sound all romantic and spoke of the lovely couples on board. He described the evening poetically and also urged us to enjoy the music.

The music was wonderful and they served some snacks on board. Some couples swayed to the slow music that was playing. It all felt like a dream.

We watched the couples dance and clapped at the end of each song.

Aadi held my hand across the table. 'Goa seems to suit you. Your skin is glowing,' he said.

'Thanks,' I smiled.

What happened next changed my life forever. The DJ called out for us, 'Can I have the handsome couple at the corner table to please come to the dais and dance?' and gave a big inviting grin.

'Us? No, no!' I blushed.

'Come on. You will love it!' Aadi pulled me up and walked me to the dais.

They played *Kiss the Girl from Blue Lagoon*. Aadi was smooth on his legs and danced to the beats. He hummed the lines as he danced and teased me as I stood there, self-consciously smiling, clapping and swaying.

As the song unwound itself, the other couples got up and danced as well. Aadi looked very happy and danced like there was no one around. With a smile he held my hand in one hand and grabbed my waist with the other and pulled me closer. He moved his hand in my hair as we swayed. I had never seen him in such a romantic mood. I guess it was the song. It seemed like he was into it. Also, there were some Western couples heating up the place.

He moved me on the dais like I was a doll, and without my knowledge we danced like we were one.

As the song gathered its momentum, everyone around who were familiar with the song sang along. As if in a trance and cheered by the crowd, Aadi bent over and kissed me on the lips.

My heart thumped loudly. *Was it a dream?* I thought. I was faint. My whole body seemed to have lost its balance. I was in his grip. I felt swept off my feet and like I was floating. It took a few seconds for me to react to what was happening. Quick! I had to do something. I had to end the euphoria before I couldn't get back. I acted. I pushed him away rather abruptly. Aadi, still in a trance, did not expect that.

I freed myself as the song ended and I bowed to the audience awkwardly and got back to the table. Aadi joined me. 'Saachi, did I do any wrong? I am sorry if I hurt you. You look so beautiful and your skin is so soft and the song... I got carried away,' Aadi said.

I maintained silence till the cruise touched the shore. Aadi apologized all through. I did not want to cry in front of the other guests. Ideally, it was a great moment between us. But not when I knew it didn't have a future.

As we got off the cruise I tried to race down. But he held my hand and dragged me to a calm place on the beach. By now I was in tears. It was dark and the moon was out, smiling. It didn't care what mood I was in. It was a full moon night. We could see each other in the moonlight.

Aadi looked at me, held my face in his hands and said, 'Saachi, I am sorry. I didn't mean to hurt you. Don't get me wrong. Please don't cry.'

'Aadi, you have to realize that I have feelings too. You say all kinds of things that a boy tells a girl when he is in love, and then say you don't mean anything, and today, you...you kissed me,' I raised my voice.

'I am sorry. Please don't be angry. I am all messed up. God! I am so confused. I don't know what to say and how to start and what I want. Saachi, you have to give me a chance to explain,' he said.

I sat down on the sand. 'Take your time. I am listening.' I desperately wanted to hear him out, and yet I still didn't know, after all these years, just what he felt. I wasn't sure and a woman needs to feel sure.

He dropped down on the sand. He looked into my eyes for a few seconds. I turned my face. He held my hands. I freed them.

'Saachi, please don't make it difficult for me. As it is, I am like a spider caught in its own web.'

'What is freaking you out so much? Why is it so difficult for you to talk it out?'

Aadi slowly turned to sit facing me now. He cupped my face with his hands.

'Saachi, I can't forget the day I saw you in Baker's Nest. You looked so nice. Something in me changed the minute I saw you.'

He then sat with his legs stretched out and looked around helplessly. He then rubbed his eyes in nervousness, looked down and then let out a deep sigh.

He slowly looked up. 'Then we met in the rain. When I spoke to you it was effortless. Everything about you is appealing to me. I can't imagine my life without you. It is not you. It is the word "Love" I am afraid of.'

'What are you afraid of? Love can never be terrifying. If it is terrifying there is something wrong,' I said calmly. He had to spit it out today.

'Saachi, it is my parents,' he said slowly.

'They were so madly in love with each other. Theirs was an arranged marriage but they came across as the most romantic couple. My dad always made it a point to take us out on holidays, in spite of his business, and spent a lot of time with my mom and me. Sometimes, I felt he loved my mom more than me. My mom's world revolved around my dad. To cut it short, they were the best pair I had seen. They both complemented each other in spite of their differences.' He paused.

I dared not interrupt.

'Looks like God doesn't like happily ever after kind of stories. We lost Mom in an accident.' Tears trickled down his face.

'My dad was grief-stricken. He would not even talk to me. Ahalya Aunty helped me cope. My dad would come back from office and lock himself in his room. He just immersed himself in work. This went on for six months. Everyone was very worried for him.' He looked pale now.

I knew this would be difficult for Aadi. But if he continued to shut it down and not share it, it would be worse.

Aadi continued, 'Then, one fine day, he came up to me and spoke. Asked me what I was up to, what my plans for the future were, that sort of thing. I was glad to have that conversation. I saw Dad had started getting back to his old self again. He seemed livelier now. We were happy for him.' He paused again.

'Three years ago I realized the reason for his change. He had another woman in his life. I saw him at Café Paradise with her,' Aadi said.

For a minute I recollected that evening I saw his dad with Niharika.

'How do you know?' I said.

'What is there to know? It was so obvious. I saw him holding her. She was crying. How could my father do this? I was happy that he was out of that intense period of grief. But it was horrendous to know it was because of another woman. Is this how much he loved my mom? Was she so easy to replace? Is this all love is about, Saachi? Why should one get married? Why can't we just spend time with someone we love?' he asked passionately.

'Have you ever confronted him about her?' I asked cautiously.

'No, he is my dad. The norm is dads catch their sons with girlfriends. Here, it is the other way round. Gosh! It is so embarrassing.'

'Aadi, first of all, I think you are jumping to conclusions. You don't even know what the actual truth is. Next, even if he had a woman in his life, what is wrong?' I said.

'What do you mean...?' I cut him short before he could complete his sentence.

'Wait. Please hear me out. Aadi, humans of all ages need company, especially when you grow old. Company can be in the form of father, mother, brother, friend, sister, anyone. It is whom you are most comfortable with and can be yourself.' I paused.

'I understand it is not easy for you to accept your dad being in a relationship with someone else. We are still not that broad-minded. But tell me, why are you so close to me and tell me stuff which you do not tell your other friends? Simply because you need someone on your own wave-length to offload and refresh. Everybody needs someone. Why are relationships judged in such a bad light? He has not done any wrong for you to lose hope in love. You have been living with this for three years? Why don't you talk it out with him like a man?'

'I don't know, Saachi. What you say is true. But it is difficult for me to accept,' Aadi said.

'Tell me, Aadi, has he ever neglected you since?' I asked.

'No. In fact, I have been doing that. I have not been very nice to him,' said Aadi.

'Doesn't he come home to you every day?' I asked.

Yes. He always comes home when I am there, when I am not there.'

'Then what is the problem? If he wants a life don't you think he deserves to get one? You don't want marriage but want to be in a relationship. Aadi, do you think I will always be around for you, like now? I need to move on. I will get married some day and have a family of my own. Things will change, Aadi,' I said.

'You want to get married?' he asked.

'Of course! Not now, but yeah, some day! May be two to three years down the line,' I said.

'Whom will you marry?' He looked dazed.

'Someone who loves me,' I said.

'What about someone whom you love?' he asked.

'What are you getting at, Aadi?' I was angry.

'Nothing. Forget it. You are right. Marriage or no marriage, I definitely need my dad to answer a few questions.' He got up and dusted his pants.

He took out his cell and made a call.

'You are calling him now?' I asked.

'Don't you think I waited too long? You never know. I may not feel like doing it again,' he said, as he walked forward.

I sat back and let him go. He was now at a distance and I could not hear him talk. His back faced me. I looked at the moon. *Why can't life be straight?* I thought. It seems God likes to complicate stuff and have fun at our cost. But then, what would life be if everything worked the way we wanted it to. There would be no surprises and no hopes of anything new.

Aadi spoke for a while. When he walked back his face looked calm. He came back and sat beside me. He was silent for a couple of minutes. Then he spoke in a very soft voice like he understood. There was acceptance in his voice now, a sense of surrender.

'He said she is just a friend. She was his friend in college before he met Mom. Both of them got out of touch later. He said he met her again accidentally after Mom passed away. She was going through a rough patch and had filed for a divorce after being married for twenty-five years. He stood by her as she had no support, and in turn, he also finds it easy to talk about the problems in his life with her because he has known her for such a long time. He even said she wants to meet me.' He sighed.

'He agreed that if I am uncomfortable with him meeting her every other day, like they do now, in public places, he'll stop meeting her. He stopped.

'What did you say?' I asked.

'I said I was sorry for having judged him and being cross with him for so many years. That he had every right to have a best friend. Why should I judge their friendship on gender? I am so relieved now, Saachi. What you said earlier is on my mind. Why was I so embarrassed? I was such a hypocrite!' he said, sounding surprised.

'Forget it, Aadi. It happens. With love comes possessiveness also. But we should know where to draw a line and not suffocate the other person. They say relationships are like holding sand in your palms. If you make a fist and try to hold the sand tight, it slips out; if you open your palms wide, the wind will blow the sand away. You have to cup your hands to hold it in place.'

'Are you an engineering student or did you study philosophy?' He hit me playfully and ran across the sand, his arms stretched wide. He was happy. A big load was off his chest, after a long long time.

The waves played hide and seek with the shore and the wind was soothing. We could hear music play in one of the shacks at a distance. It was the best holiday of my life so far.

Slowly Aadi stopped, turned and walked towards me, calming down. He fell on his knees, held my hand and whispered, 'Saachi, I am crazy about you. I love everything about you. I can't forget the first day I saw you. You have such clear eyes. I like your smile. I love the way you pull my leg. I love the way you care. I love it when you hold me on my bike. I love it when you shiver in the cold and wrap your hands around you. I love the way you look when you are wet in the rain and water drips from your hair. I love the way you eat bhutta. I love the way you are carefree in front of me. I love your voice on the phone. I love your husky sleepy voice in the morning. I love you, Saachi, more than anything else in this world. I forget the world when you are around me. There is magic in the air. I have never felt so passionate about anyone before. You don't know how difficult it was for me to hide my love or whatever I thought it was, that special feeling towards you,' he looked into my eyes.

My hands and feet turned cold. I could not believe he said that.

'Are you proposing to me?' I asked, looking into his eyes.

'You have every right to say no,' he said, as he got up and took my upper lip between his lips. He then kissed my lower lip. The kiss was tender in the beginning and grew more and more passionate every second. I felt faint. I surrendered.

The waves washed away the sand beneath our legs. We looked into each other's eyes as he released me.

He sat back on his knees and said, 'Saachi, will you marry me?'

'I will marry you, if you promise that each kiss of our life will be as passionate as our first one,' I replied dreamily, as I sat on his knee.

'Let me try,' he said, as he reached for my lips and we kissed again.

Aadi had found an anchor. I had found the wind which would help me sail.

Later, Riya told me that Manish had got back before us. He found Riya sitting on her balcony all by herself. She had been crying. Manish sat beside her on the comfortable bean-bag.

'Riya,' Manish said softly. Riya had sensed someone come as she heard footsteps.

She looked at Manish and wiped her tears. 'Hi. Did you meet your friend?'

'Yes. His house was beside a well-known chapel. It was easy to find,' he spoke casually.

Riya fell silent. When she spoke she said, 'Sorry, Manish.'

'For what?' Manish asked.

'You know for what!'

'You know what, Riya, I would be most hurt if you are sorry about us. Don't be. Buddy, at the end of the day, the truth is we will be there for each other till our last breath. That is a promise from my side, at least. What more can we ask for? Isn't such a relationship above anything else in the world?'

Manish made sense and he was at ease saying that.

Riya nodded. 'I love you,' she said, as she got up and hugged him.

Manish said, 'Same here,' and kissed her forehead. Their love was selfless, without expectations and with respect for each other.

Riya slowly recovered with time from the aftermath of a relationship gone sour. It was definitely not easy for her. There were many nights when she wept herself to sleep. There were mornings when she woke up to feel emptiness in her life. Many times she had dreams of Vidit pushing her into the deep ocean. There were times when she thought in vain that may be, if she had done something different, Vidit would still be in her life. There were times when she cursed her fate for the tattered bonds in her life. There were times when she regretted being attracted to him in the first place. Nonetheless, what matters is she survived through all her weak moments and looked forward to what life had in store for her.

Five Years Later

I awoke from an afternoon nap. My mom was reading a letter. My dad was busy on the phone making arrangements for my marriage.

'Saachi, you have received your appointment letter from the firm in Pune.' She was excited.

'Wow. Give that to me,' I said, as I plucked the letter from her hand.

I had to join in a month. After college I worked for three years in IT and realized I was a people's person. So I decided the apt thing to do with myself was to get an MBA in HR. I was very happy doing that. Aadi was now settled in Pune and had set up his own automobiles business. He was very successful and loved what he did.

Aadi's dad shuttled between Pune and Bengaluru. Niharika and Ahalya Aunty were making all the arrangements for our marriage.

We had decided on a simple wedding and a grand reception in a hotel. Aadi made sure that my dad spent only for the wedding, and he hosted the reception with his own money.

I got a call from Riya. 'Babe, Mathew and I are taking the flight day after tomorrow from Dubai. Did you check out the bridal-wear designs I sent? I will get to work as soon as I get there. Your dresses should be ready within a week. I am so happy, Saachi. I can't believe you are getting married.' Her voice was very excited on the other end.

Riya had moved to London with her mom. She also took up a two-year course in fashion designing while she worked with her mom in her boutique. Her mom had changed in leaps and bounds and was a more secure and sane person now. Riya travelled the globe and promoted the Pereira designer-wear label. She met Mathew, an advertising guy, on one of her tours. He was European. They hit it off instantly. She had been seeing him for the last three years. She was deciding to move in with him, but had ruled out marriage.

I called Aadi to give him the good news of my job.

'Hi, best friend,' he said.

'Aadi, I got the job. So I am going to work. Get ready to cook,' I said.

'That is so much better. Imagine eating the food you cook. I'd rather starve,' he said. 'I'll retire and make you earn. I'd love to be a house-husband.

'So, what plans for the evening?' he asked.

'Lingerie shopping,' I said.

'Wow! Can you wait till I get there?'

'Shut up!' I said.

'On our first night, make sure there are strawberries all over your lingerie,' he laughed.

'Aadi, looks like we're going to get divorced before marriage,' I threatened.

'Okay. What about cherries?' he said.

'They have colours and designs. Not flavours,' I laughed.

Next morning Manish and Manvi visited me. Manish had moved to the US to complete his MS. There he met Manvi who was a lecturer. She was five years older to him. He fell for her maturity and wisdom. He proposed to her after studies. They both decided to move back to India after marriage, and started a school which both of them jointly manage. Manvi was now five months pregnant.

'Riya is coming tomorrow. Did she call you?' Manish asked.

'Yes. I am going to meet Mathew for the first time. Also, she wants to design all my bridal wear!'

'Did I tell you I bumped into Vidit at a mall?' Manish said.

'Really! How is he?' I was curious. All the memories came flooding back.

'He is good. He is engaged. I met his fiancée as well. He has settled for an arranged marriage. Looks like he didn't have the guts to propose to anyone after what happened.' Both of us laughed.

The next ten days were very busy with friends and relatives visiting, shopping and calls from Aadi. Riya handpicked all my dresses and made sure I looked like the best presented bride ever. For the first time Riya's mom and dad got down from the same car on the night of our reception. Mathew was a very easy-going chap and was crazy about Riya.

Manish made doubly sure that Manvi was not tired with all the wedding excitement and assisted her hand and foot.

It was the happiest day of my life, not just because I was marrying Aadi, but two of my best friends had found the loves of their life.

At our reception a wedding cake was ordered from Baker's Nest and a pair of doves stood on the cake.

My parents, Aadi's dad, Niharika, Ahalya Aunty, Riya's parents were all looking very happy and welcomed the guests.

Aadi looked handsome in a tuxedo and I wore a lehnga designed by Riya.

Aadi said, 'Hi beautiful!' when he met me on the dais. I pinched myself to make sure that the moment was true and not a dream.

The evening was filled with laughter, cheer and happiness. Aadi kept pulling my leg all evening at every moment he got a chance.

Riya and Mathew came to drop us off at the airport. We had decided to spend our week-long honeymoon in Goa at the Pereira Beach Resort.

The penthouse was decorated with lilies and red roses and candles were lit all through. It was better than I had imagined. I wore cherry-coloured lingerie as Aadi had wished. He stood in the balcony looking at the moon while he waited for me to step out of the dressing room.

Light music played in the background. I walked up to him and hugged him from behind.

I whispered, 'Aadi, I love you.'

He turned, lifted me in his arms and carried me into the room.

'Saachi, I love this life because you are a part of it. I have been dreaming of this day for a long time,' said Aadi, as he gently put me on the bed.

We made love and it felt blissful to lie all night in the arms of the man I was so much in love with. Aadi cuddled me and slept peacefully.

I fell asleep dreaming of what a laugh riot it would be to be married to the best friend of my life.

Acknowledgements

ᘓ

You alone are never responsible for anything good, bad or ugly that happens. This book would not have been possible without my partners-in-crime.

My first thanks goes to my two-year-old brat, Vihaan, who showed immense patience as I went rat-tat-tat on my keyboard. Vihaan, I love you for being so surprisingly mature for your age. You are a Godsend.

I will be forever grateful to my parents, who have always centered their life around me.

A high-five to Amit, supposedly my husband but more of a friend, who, even after a long day's work would sit patiently and read my drafts.

My book would not have happened without the support of my best admirer and worst critic, Sushmitha, who read and re-read my draft and gave it a good shape. It is amazing how she managed my book as well as her two-year-old. Her dedication to this book surpassed my own.

Bear hugs to my BFF, Madhu, who always makes me laugh and brings out the goofy in me. Being the first person to know that I was thinking of penning a book, he said with blind faith that I could do anything if I wanted to. Thanks, Madhu, for it is friends like you who keep me going.

My love to Sudha, who helps me conquer my worst fears. She has always been there even without asking. There is never a dull moment with her around.

My thanks to Archana, my childhood friend, with whom I shared all my love stories. She got me hooked onto *Mills & Boon* and taught me to dream hopelessly.

I appreciate all my friends who spontaneously said 'wow!' when they heard I am writing a book.

I am grateful to Rupa Publications, who put their faith in debutants like me. Their support is priceless. I also thank the editorial team at Rupa comprising Kausalya Saptharishi and Shyama Laxman.

I bow my head to the invincible power in this universe which helps us create.

Wait! Did I thank myself for being an incurable romantic at heart?

Made in the USA
Monee, IL
07 July 2026

56550061R00111